Transformation Trance Formation

By Christian Skoorsmith, MA
Board Certified Hypnotist
Certifying Hypnosis Instructor

~ Second Edition ~
2022
WholeHealth Hypnosis
Seattle, WA

www.WholeHealth.today

First Edition Published in 2021
Second Edition Published in 2021
by WholeHealth Hypnosis
9451 35th Ave SW, Ste. 200
Seattle, WA 98126

Contents

Introduction

Another "self-help" book, really?

Look, I know what you might be thinking... because I've been there, too. I've rolled my eyes and thought: "This book has something to say that *no one else* has ever said? *This* book is going to make the difference?"

To be honest, I'm pretty sure everything in this book already existed before I thought it or wrote it down. But the reality is you are here right now, with this book in your hands, for a reason. I don't know what that reason is. (*You* may not even know – consciously – what that reason is!) But we are here together at this moment for a reason.

So let's just take a moment.

You have a mind. A beautiful mind. A mind that has extraordinary power to shape your life. It is *already* shaping your life. You behave the way you do, respond or react the way you do, move the way you do, speak the way you do, because you have a mind that has been shaped by experiences and insights throughout your life. You are as successful as you are right now because of your incredible mind.

But maybe your mind is also holding you back in some ways. Perhaps a habit, or a habitual reaction, or a nagging impostor syndrome, or a fear or worry or stress. Maybe you are simply interested in how to make yourself *even better*.

Then this little book might be a good place to start.

We take a quick dip into the psychology of why our minds our predisposed to *not* change, why change is sometimes (oftentimes?) difficult, and how we can actually *take advantage* of that. Then we lay into how the Subconscious works on a fundamental level. Once we've laid the groundwork, we go in two opposite directions:

first touring the dynamics of fear and how that grows, but then secondly flipping that around to see an example of how that same dynamic holds tremendous personal and interpersonal hope. Finally, I walk through a simple and effective way to do transformational trance-work yourself, as soon as you close the book (and close your eyes).

Now, if you want to, you can just skip to the last chapter and get started right away. That's fine. I think you'll be interested in learning more about how this whole thing works – whether before you start deliberately shaping your life or after. You don't need to know *how* it works, or *why* it works. You can just experience it working. (But why not know the *how* and *why*, too?)

I add to the end of this book some advice about looking for a professional hypnotist. Sometimes it helps to have professional help, and some guidance for what to look for might be useful. Hypnosis is a broad-ranging modality that I have found to be profoundly helpful in my own life, and in the lives of my clients. I really believe in it – when it is well-done by a skilled and ethical professional. (The task is to find such a person!)

In short, this is a quick introduction to *you* – a peek "under the hood," so to speak, at the mechanisms and dynamics that drive your engine. It is a how-to for programming yourself for the kind of life you want, to make the changes in your life and behavior that you *need* to live the life you want.

Join me on this safari, where the savanna is you. You won't be disappointed.

Chapter 1
Why We Don't Change (and How We Can)
A Model of the Mind

The following page provides a useful model of the mind. This isn't a medical model; you can't lay this over a map of the brain and say, "Here's the amygdala," and "Here's the pre-frontal cortex." It's not a model that psychologists or neuroscientists would use to talk to each other about how the brain works. It is more of an analogy, a visualization, a model to help us talk about how the mind works, and give us a place to begin our discussion.

Let us start over on the right side with the **Unconscious Mind.** The Unconscious Mind is that part of our brain that comes pre-programmed; the part that controls our body, that knows how to digest food, the part that knows how to oxygenate our blood, to fight-off infections, knows how to regulate our core temperature. We don't *learn* how to digest food, we just do it. It's also where our deepest instincts lie, like the fight-flight-freeze instinct, or when babies react to loud noises or startle if they think they are falling. That's not something babies learn, they are just born that way.

Since it comes pre-programmed, there's not a whole lot of change that can happen in this part of the brain. The scope of change is really very limited. You have probably heard of Dr. Ivan Pavlov, a Russian scientist in the first half of the 20th century, now most famous for training dogs to salivate at the sound of a bell. Through his studies on animals and humans, he developed the idea of "classical conditioning": shaping animals' and sometimes people's behavior (and even their unconscious, physical responses) using reward and punishment, and observing how this dynamic shapes so much of our lives.

3

Conscious	Critical Factor	Subconscious	Unconscious
Point of Focus	Filtering / Comparing	Starts Out Empty	"Body-Mind" Immune System, Digestion Breathing, Heart-rate
Critical Thinking		Long-Term Memory	
Will Power		Beliefs & Habits	
Short-Term Memory	Limited Capacity	Generates *Emotions*	Instincts
Limited Capacity (7-9 bits of information)		Unlimited Capacity	Limited Change Generates *Feelings*
Reasoning: Linear (Analytic, Logical)	Reasoning: Association	Reasoning: Association	Reasoning: Stimuli-Response
<u>Protects Against</u> Perceived Danger	<u>Protects Against</u> Unnecessary Changes	<u>Protects Against</u> "Known" Dangers and Motivates You to Fulfill Your Needs	<u>Protects Against</u> Infection & Injury (Using Reflexes)

4

This is still a popular and effective model for understanding human behavior and how we shape or change it. In Pavlov's footsteps is a long line of American Behaviorist psychologists. Prominent among them is B.F. Skinner who believed humans to be just a series of conditioned responses. This is a comfortable conviction for "evidence-based" theorists because it models the mind as mechanistic, a complicated repertoire of levers and gears, which makes behavior and psychology "objectively testable"... at least in the lab. Real life is often less clear-cut. This mechanistic conception, however, might be reflecting the phenomena I am locating in the Unconscious Mind.

What I am calling the Unconscious, though, is the pre-programmed, innate, instinctual, genetic material (behaviors, operations, responses, reflexes) that enables our bodies to function and survive, honed over billions of years of evolution. Since the scope of change in the Unconscious isn't really that great, we don't typically spend much time therapeutically trying to change it. The reason I bring it up in this context is because oftentimes the Subconscious *uses* the Unconscious to communicate with us.

Because the Subconscious is below conscious awareness ("sub"=below), there's not a way for it to directly break through and communicate directly with the Conscious Mind. So, oftentimes what it will do, is use our Unconscious to create feelings in our body as a way of drawing our attention to whatever it thinks our needs, wants and desires are. (In common parlance, subconscious and unconscious are used interchangeably, and mean roughly the same thing. Clearly, I am using these terms "Subconscious" and "Unconscious" in particular ways in this model, to be a little more specific about which mental phenomenon I am referring to.)

For instance, let's say you are in a given situation and your Subconscious is paying attention, as it always does, and it comes to the conclusion that you might be in some sort of danger. So, it uses your body's brain (the "Unconscious"), to create that pit in your stomach, or that tension in your chest, or the adrenaline in your arms, whatever feeling "on edge" or anxious feels like to you. Now, you *feel* anxious. You get that feeling and you become consciously aware of it, so now you can do something about it. You can get yourself out of that situation or address whatever the concern is. The Subconscious uses the Unconscious to create these feelings as a way of communicating with us.

When I work with clients, whenever we partner in this kind of insight-generating work, it's always important that my clients feel free to *feel* their feelings. As adults, we're really good at having trained ourselves not to feel our feelings, especially if those feelings are uncomfortable, or "bad." We coach ourselves with sentiments like, "Oh, that happened a long time ago," or "I shouldn't be so sensitive," or "They didn't mean that," or, "That's just them," or "I shouldn't take it so personally." Whatever the reasoning is, we try to deny it, or stuff it down, or discredit our feelings or their justification. We teach ourselves to *not* feel our feelings, to not trust them.

This isn't just as adults – most of us have been taught from a very early age that our feelings were bad. We were told, "Don't feel bad," or "Don't feel sad," "Don't be mad," "Don't cry," "Don't get angry," and so on. Over the course of our childhood we learn the lesson that our *feelings* were the problem; that we shouldn't let ourselves feel the feeling. So even as adults we deny the feelings, we ignore the feelings, we try to not feel the feelings. This is generally problematic in our lives, and we will cover this in greater detail shortly. Even more so, however, is it unhealthy when we're talking about the work that we can do in hypnosis and hypnotherapy. We want to be able to really feel our feelings because those feelings are simply what the Subconscious is using to communicate what it thinks our needs, wants, and desires are.

In my work with clients, I really want them to be able to feel those feelings, to really hold on to them, lean into those feelings; because those feelings are data, information. All of our feelings are good in the sense that they are information. We will be coming back to this idea in more detail, but it is important to keep in mind. *All of our feelings are good, even the bad ones, even the uncomfortable ones, the unpleasant ones, the ones we'd rather not feel. All of those feelings are good because all of them are information about what our Subconscious thinks our needs, wants, and desires are.*

These feelings are like the end of a thread. If we can just hold on to the end of that thread long enough, we can actually trace that back into the Subconscious and figure out what at root is going on there. Once we respond satisfactorily to that need, once we've addressed that underlying issue, then that feeling has done its work and it fades away. Sometimes we do this in hypnosis, but it is also something we can do in our everyday life. It is a skill that can be developed and strengthened, that allows us to *listen* to our feelings. They are telling us something important. For me, that is the important thing to know about the Unconscious Mind, our body's brain.

The Subconscious is that part of our mind that, when we're born, is virtually empty. We start collecting experiences, and for the first five to seven years of our lives we are in a permanent state of hypnosis. When we are that young we don't have any previous experiences to compare with these new experiences we are having, so we just accept everything at face value. This is the reason I could believe in things like Santa Claus: somebody at some point told me Santa Claus exists, and I had no reason to not believe them, so... okay, Santa Claus exists. This is also how we learn how gravity works: we just keep dropping things until we figure it out. It is how we learn how our limbs move, how language works, how facial expressions work. It is how we learn about ourselves ("I like lasagna," or "I don't like lasagna"), about our place in the world, about relationships, about how the world works.

Our mind takes these individual experiences, these points of information, and connects the dots, so we can understand the world and ourselves. We can predict how things are going or how to respond appropriately. We connect these dots pretty quickly. Soon, our mind is able to gather enough information that we start building understandings about the world: "truths" we "know" about the world, what we can expect from it, and what we understand things to mean. (I put "truth" and "know" in quotes here, because there is no objective knowledge in the Subconscious – it is all subjective knowledge, just our assumptions, our conclusions, based on our interpretations about our experiences. One of the cruel, but unavoidable, ironies of being human is that we form most of our fundamental assumptions about the world at a time when we are least able to make really good assumptions about the world, when we have the least experience and understanding.)

We start building a bank of all these truths, these scripts, these beliefs and understandings. Then these scripts, these understandings, start to affect how we see the world. They shape how we encounter the world, how we process our experiences. Any new experience has to fit into one of these existing files, these programs, these understandings about how the world works. We shoe-horn any new experience into how we already understand the world to work.

At this point, I'm making the Subconscious sound a little manipulative. But really, the Subconscious is an evolutionary adaptation. The whole point of the Subconscious is that once you *learn* something, you don't have to *re*-learn it. Like tying your shoes or taking a shower or making breakfast, or language or facial expressions, or your spouse's birthday or parents' anniversary, driving a car, language. Once you learn these things, you don't have to re-learn them. You can spend your time and attention, your focus and your energy, learning something new. It is part of the genius of our species.

But what happens when one of those things we know to be true ends up being false, or maladaptive, or unhelpful, or even just contrary to the way you wanna live your life? How do we change those subconscious scripts when the whole point of the Subconscious is that it doesn't change?

That's the central question we're dealing with here, so hold on to it for just a moment and we'll circle back around to it.

Let us look briefly at the **Conscious Mind**. Skip over the Critical Factor for just a moment and talk about the Conscious Mind. The Conscious Mind is that part of our mind that is like a laser: it's super powerful, but only when it's really focused. Like a laser, we now know that if that conscious attention gets too diffused, it loses a lot of its power and effectiveness. Through the past thirty years or so of cognitive science, we know that the human mind can only hold on to seven-to-nine pieces of information at a time. More than that and we start losing bits of information. What we also now know is that it is not just limited in terms of focus; it is also limited in terms of duration and volume. Attention-energy is a finite resource that you can deplete, that you can run out of over the course of the day. It is one of those things that gets recharged when you're sleeping at night. It is why, generally, we make better decisions in the morning than we do in the evening, because we have more of that decision-making power.

There was a good article on this several years ago, when Obama was President. Apparently, Obama had only two suits in his closet: a black one and a dark blue one. An interviewer pointed out "You're the President of the United States. You really should have more than two suits." Obama replied with something to the effect of: "I have so many decisions to make in a day, I'm not going to waste any of that energy on what I should wear. So I just pick one, and whatever happens that day, that is what I'm wearing – whether meeting a foreign dignitary or playing in the Rose Garden." The article went on to talk about decision-making ability, and how it was a psychologically limited resource in the mind. The energy it takes to make good decisions could get depleted over the course of a day, or even a few minutes of stress.

A lot of my weight loss clients really resonate with this idea. In the morning, they are committed to the diet, they have a good breakfast, they pack a good lunch. Then, over the course of the day, because of crappy customers or co-workers, bills, traffic, kids, spouses, politics... whatever it is, they just get worn down. Then they are driving home and it is as if they go on auto pilot. All of a sudden they find themselves driving into the drive-through lane. They hear themselves ordering what they know they shouldn't be eating. They know they are going to eat it, because when the Conscious Mind has enough energy, it is driving the bus. But when the Conscious runs out of steam, they fall back on all those subconscious scripts, and somewhere in there is one of those scripts that says, "Eat that hamburger. It's gonna make you feel better." Or, "Eat that ice cream. It will make you feel validated... at least for a few minutes."

What makes this whole process possible, is this thing called the **Critical Factor**, sometimes called the Critical Faculty. The Critical Factor is not a place in the brain as much as it is a function of the mind. It is that critical, weighing, comparing, *filtering* mechanism that takes any new incoming experience (from "outside" or even our own self-talk), and compares it with all of the things we know to be true: all of those scripts, those programs, those lessons and expectations that are so old they feel like the truth. If that new experience corresponds with what we already know to be true, it passes right through that filter and goes into the Subconscious Mind, goes into one of those files, and your mind says, "See, I told you so..." But if it *conflicts* with what you already know to be true, and it seems significant, that Critical Factor will capture that idea and put it in a sort of holder file of contrary evidence with the reasonable expectation that if that file ever gets big enough, then you'll have to reconsider one of your previously held beliefs.

But let's face it, that hardly ever happens, because every tiny little thing is going into those files, re-confirming what you already think you know to be true, what you are predisposed to believe. It is how confirmation bias works, why prejudice exists: it is an efficiency of the mind, an energy-saving maneuver that sorts things into categories of resemblance or association so we can understand them (or think we understand them) more quickly, more easily. The mind reinforces those over and over and over again.

Hardly ever do we get enough contrary evidence to really unseat one of those previously held beliefs. One of the few times this consciously happened in my own life is when I stopped believing in Santa Claus. At some point that file got big enough. I started figuring things out. The kids at school were talking about it. I noticed that Santa's handwriting looked a lot like Mom's handwriting. Santa Claus' shoes looked like Dad's shoes. I started putting it together and eventually I came to the point where I just couldn't believe it anymore. I have to give it up.

So I decide Santa Claus does not exist and I switch out that belief. Now, in my mind, there's the certainty that Santa Claus does *not* exist. Part of that belief, however, is the subconscious understanding that everyone I know and trust has been lying to me for years. What *else* have they been lying to me about?! What about the Tooth Fairy? What about the Easter Bunny? What about when they said they loved me? When they said that I was safe? What about when they said that they'd be home at night?

My brain had to re-negotiate all of those relationships, to figure out what I could trust and what I couldn't. And that takes a lot of energy. It's traumatic in itself! That process takes a lot of psychological energy, and so our mind learns really quickly that we don't want to have that happen very often. So the Critical Factor serves to *protect* and *privilege* everything we think we know to be true; essentially, to keep it from changing unless it absolutely has to change. Which brings us back to that central question: how do we change the Subconscious, how do we reprogram those scripts, those truths, that underlying programming, when the whole system is rigged to keep them from changing?

There are typically three ways to change the subconscious. The first is through trauma. **Trauma** can rewrite the Subconscious really quickly. Most of us likely don't need an example, but a somewhat humorous illustration from my own life might help. It was my first really bad alcohol-related experience in college. I was at a party and a friend of mine had a bottle of Amaretto. Amaretto is a sweet, almond-based liqueur. I'd never had it before. And it's delicious. Now, this was my first real experience with hard liquor, and no one had ever talked to me about sipping. Since it tasted like a milkshake, I drank it like a milkshake. You can imagine the rest of the story, so I'll just skip to the end where I am sicker than I'd ever been. I'm there violently retching in the bathroom, I thought I was gonna die, and all I could taste was Amaretto.

From that one experience, that one traumatic night (probably only about an hour and-a-half), now for the rest of my life, if I even smell Amaretto I get sick to my stomach. That file, that program, that association is deeply written in my Subconscious. As soon as I sniff Amaretto – I don't think about it – I want to throw up. Now, intellectually, I know that Amaretto does not pose a threat to my health or warrant such a reaction, but subconsciously there's that experience. My Subconscious

13

gets the Amaretto-signal and connects to that experience in college and says, "I know what to do about this!" Then my Subconscious uses my Unconscious (body-brain) to create that sick feeling in my stomach so I don't go down that road again.

Trauma can rewrite the subconscious really quickly, but it's not a very kind therapeutic technique, and so I don't rely on it in my practice.

More broadly than just "trauma," we could point to any kind of emotionally-charged experience; it doesn't necessarily have to be negative. Falling in love is a similar kind of emotional experience that re-wires our brains in surprising and stubbornly persistent ways. How many of us know someone who seems entirely unable to see the faults in the object of their love? Love is blind because we filter all subsequent experience through the lens of those first few associations we attached to that person. Many of those associations might have been created and cultivated long before we even met the other person, and we unconsciously glombed them onto our beloved. Our expectations or interpretative lens might be profoundly inaccurate, but it typically takes a long time and a lot of contrary experiences to crack the nut of our preconceived idea of who someone is… which brings us to another way to change subconscious programming.

The second way to change the Subconscious is through a repeated, protracted **experience** – doing the same thing over and over and over again. This is what I think most of us mean when we talk about "changing our habits." But this is also what professional athletes do when they practice the same lay-up shot, or the same tennis swing over and over and over again. We call it "muscle memory," but really it is simply training the Subconscious to do that exact, correct physical movement, allowing the Conscious Mind to concentrate on everything else on the court. So it is a very effective and legitimate technique. It works.

The problem though, is how do we *not* do something over and over again? It's kind of like asking one to *not* think of a pink elephant. As soon as we read that sentence, we thought on some level of a pink elephant. We hadn't thought of a pink elephant for weeks or months, probably, maybe even for several years. But the mere mention brings it up in our mind. Even if I said, *don't* think of a pink elephant, all of a sudden we're now thinking of a pink elephant, and somehow weirdly try to push it out of our mind. Bringing up the thing that we don't want to remember actually causes us to remember it. Even saying, "Don't focus on it," at least for a moment or two, actually makes us focus on it, and we end up reinforcing the thing that we intended not to reinforce.

This repetitive strategy works. It is one of the most-studied phenomena in human learning. It goes back at least to Russian psychologist Ivan Pavlov and his famously salivating dogs. This "classical conditioning" also dominated American psychology for fifty years or so in the wake of B. F. Skinner and others in the mid-20th century. It is still a potent force in research and education. Because of this "pink elephant" phenomenon, however, it is only so helpful at *un*-learning subconscious beliefs. At best, we would only be substituting some new stimulus for an old one. Sometimes that's enough to solve the problem, but for most of our deeper issues it seems more like a band-aid that leaves the underlying wound unhealed.

A third way to change the Subconscious is through hypnosis. **Hypnosis** is a natural state of mind, a phenomenon that we experience many times a day, every day of our lives. It is really just a deep learning state, when we are simply more open to suggestion. Hypnosis is what we call it when the Critical Factor moves off to the side for a moment and allows the Conscious Mind and the Subconscious Mind to interact and re-program. (You never "lose" the Critical Factor; it isn't ever completely "removed," even temporarily.) Then, when you come out of hypnosis, that Critical Factor comes back in again, now protecting the *new* programming in the same way that it had protected the old.

This happens to us many times a day. It happens if we're ever reading a really good book. If it's a really good book, we *forget* we're reading a book. An hour could go by and we don't remember turning a page. We don't remember reading a paragraph. All we remember is the story. It is alive in our mind where, in reality, we are just looking at ink marks on a page.

When I was newly married, my wife's favorite book was Jane Austen's *Pride and Prejudice*, that classic romance set in Regency-period England. So, I needed to read *Pride and Prejudice* in order to understand my wife a little better. I would read it at bedtime – when I was half in hypnosis anyway – and after a couple of weeks I noticed that I was speaking strangely. Throughout my day, I would say things that would sound strange, but I couldn't figure out what was wrong with what I was saying. One evening I was reading the book and I realized that I had started to speak in Regency-period English. I had started to speak like the characters in that book. Because I was in that state of hypnosis while reading, those characters' speech patterns started to re-write my speech patterns, and it was bubbling out spontaneously in my daily life unconsciously, unintentionally throughout my day.

This also happens when we're watching a really good movie. Again, if it's a good movie, we forget we're watching a movie. Now, it isn't as if it is "me" in the movie. It is simply that, for that time, *that story* is the only thing that exists. It is so good, we let that suggested reality simply wash over us.

Now, if somebody plucked us out of the theater and said, "You do realize you're in a dark room with a bunch of strangers?" We would of course know that. If they said: "You know that's a two-dimensional screen; that world doesn't exist." We would nod. Yes, of course, we know that. "And those people you see, those are actors who are being paid to say lines that somebody else wrote!" Yes, I know that. "And the music is specifically choreographed to manipulate your emotions. You realize that, right?" Yes, *of course*, I know that. But I don't *care!* It's such a good story. I just let that suggested reality wash over me. For that period of time, because all those objections aren't getting in the way of us immersing ourselves in the experience *as if it were true*, we are in a light state of hypnosis.

What I love about that example is this. When we finish watching an engrossing movie and we leave the theater, we still feel like we're (sort of) *in that world*. If we spend two hours watching *Harry Potter*, say, afterwards we still feel kind of *magical*. Or if we spend two hours in a spy thriller, we leave feeling bold and adventurous, limber and exciting, and that the world is conspiratorial, fast-paced and exciting. If we spend two hours watching Star Wars, as we're driving home from the theater, part of us is driving down the interstate and part of our mind is flying the Millennium Falcon. Back in 1999, everyone walked out of the first Matrix movie in unsettled awe, curious whether they were in an elaborate computer program, and how they'd ever know.

Because we were in a light state of hypnosis, that worldview started to re-program our subconscious expectations about reality. Because we were in hypnosis, its influence *carried on* after that initial experience. But, of course, those are silly suggestions: we aren't really magical, international spies, or space-travelling buccaneers. So those suggestions wear off pretty quickly.

But let's say you were in an experience where, for the first time in forty years, you were a non-smoker. You leave that experience and it comes time in the day where, in the past, you would have had a cigarette. Now, there are two scripts playing in your mind. One that says, "I'm a smoker, go get that cigarette, it'll make me feel better." And another that says, "Wait, I'm a non-smoker now, why would I do that? Smoking is gross, or disgusting, or expensive, or unhealthy, or yellows my teeth, or smells bad..." (whatever the reasoning is... maybe all of them!). Now you get to *choose* between the two reactions or behaviors – and the one you choose gets *stronger*, and the one you don't starts to wither away. It is always easier to make that choice when you have a strong alternative already deeply programmed in there. *That's* what hypnosis is able to do for us.

We aren't ever automatons under someone else' control. In hypnosis we don't lose our good judgment or sense of morals. There is always a part of us looking out for our best interests. Once, when my wife and I were experimenting with hypnosis and exploring different styles and products, we tried a recorded direct-suggestion session on "abundance." We thought abundance meant a sense of personal belonging and security, more along the lines of confidence and resilience – but the hypnotist intended to talk about *money*. My wife and I were in deep, really enjoying it, when the hypnotist mentioned wealth or money, and started talking about abundance as an *economic* value. Both my wife and I mentioned after the session that it was *that* point when we both were suddenly and spontaneously very aware of what we were doing, and of what the hypnotist was saying – because it didn't align with our values or expectations. We had effectively "emerged" from hypnosis.

When we *want* the suggestions, however, when they are in alignment with our goals and intentions and values (whether it is to quit smoking or cluck like a chicken at a stage show), our minds are *open* to those suggestions. When we *want* to make the right choice, but feel like we've been hamstrung by old habits, thought-patterns, or beliefs, hypnosis can help us re-program ourselves to lean toward the behaviors and thoughts we *want*, rather than those we don't. We always have the freedom to choose, but we want our heart to have our brain's back, so to speak, and not "sabotage" our best intentions.

In another important sense, "want" has to be more than in the Conscious Mind. Many of my smoking cessation clients *want* to quit smoking. Yet most of them admit to also *not* wanting to quit. Even those who are steadfastly resolved to quit still struggle – that's why they come to see a hypnotist. Oftentimes what clients discover is that they want to *want* to change. Some part of them sees poor behavior as the *right* choice, as answering some need, as *helping* somehow. The task of hypnosis is often simply getting all these disparate parts of the mind to be on the same page, to play for the same side, to lean in the same direction.

Psychological research since the 1960s has revealed that what we experience as conscious choice is actually pre-consciously or unconsciously determined before we "make" the decision. Some part outside of conscious awareness decides (sometimes as much as a full half-second beforehand) and then the Conscious Mind experiences itself as choosing. Without exploring this fascinating and well-documented research, let us draw a preliminary conclusion that affirms how important it is to lay pre-conscious/unconscious/subconscious programming that facilitates our making the choices we *want* to choose.

In a real sense, *all* of these (trauma/emotion, repeated experiences, and formal "hypnosis") are examples of hypnosis: when the critical filter of our mind is open to receiving new information... essentially when we are *learning* anything. We don't typically call it "hypnosis" – we just think of it as being human. There are many ways to "induce" hypnosis: relaxation, *almost* falling asleep, boredom, anxiety, stress, surprise, overloading the critical factor with too much information too quickly, and so on. I will discuss some of these in coming chapters of this book.

It should be clearer now why our minds find change so difficult. We are programmed, *hardwired* by evolution, to resist change. Our brains are designed to conserve energy, and learning takes more energy than already knowing. It is what confirmation bias is; why prejudice exists. How this was advantageous in our evolution as a species can be seen in a simple thought experiment.

Imagine some cave-people ancestors of ours walking merrily along when they come upon a Saber-tooth tiger. Imagine there are two kinds of ancestors here. One carefully considered all the imaginable variables, the long and short-term ramifications and implications and possibilities of these options. Maybe this tiger is different than the last one. What would my spouse think if I brought this home? Maybe it isn't hungry? Which path should I take? Is a spear or a sling going to be better? Maybe the sun is in its eyes and it can't see me. And so on.

The other ancestor went immediately into "lantern consciousness," becoming uncritically aware of the situation and relying on instincts and prior experience to make a decision about what to do – fight, flee, freeze, or play dead. Get my spear up or run? Run!

One of these ancestors did not survive to pass on their genes – the calm, considered, critical-thinking one – because they were *eaten by the tiger*. They took too long in careful consideration when they needed to act immediately. Our survival depended in certain situations on the ability to suspend our higher thinking and rely on more basic programming: those experiences or assumptions that are so old they feel like the truth.

This ability to rely on prior experience is also advantageous in lots of other ways: we don't have to re-learn how to tie our shoes, how to drive a car, how to speak our language, how to make breakfast. We are empowered by our Subconscious Mind to focus on more interesting things. It is, as I said earlier, the genius of our species. (It is present to some extent in most species, especially mammals and pronouncedly among primates. It can be demonstrated, again, with classical conditioning: that Pavlovian dog-trick associating a bell with food and leading to salivation.)

It is also, however, frustratingly stubborn, as we have seen in recent years highlighting implicit bias among well-meaning people who would never "consciously" be racist, sexist, or given to wildly unsupported conspiracy theories.

So, all of the foregoing is simply to lay out how difficult it is for us to really, deeply *change* (and why), and also to point to the way(s) in which we *can*. For all our deep programming and hard-wiring *against* change, we are also deeply wired *for* change. Change, adaptation, and the ability to incorporate new understanding and novel information *is* the genius of our species. It might take us a while, and we often don't even realize we are resisting it, until we've already made the change. Arthur Schopenhauer wrote: "All truth passes through three stages: First, it is ridiculed; second, it is violently opposed; third, it is accepted as self-evident." This makes sense among individuals (as a society or group) and also *within* individuals. We all wrestle with new insights and challenging points of view, at some point coming to the conclusion that this new way of thinking is self-evident.

Being able to *shape* that process, *direct* it or encourage it to go in a particular direction or end in a particular place, is the *real* task of learning, of self-work, of enlightenment. It might be what we mean by *insight*.

Chapter 2
Resonance – the Hidden Hum of Our Daily Lives

Have you ever overreacted? I mean, like out-of-the-blue lost it, without even realizing why you were so upset? Sure, whatever happened sucked, but the level of anger, anxiety, fear, sadness or frustration you felt wasn't really appropriate to how sort-of-bad that one situation or "thing" was, right? Sure, we've all been there.
Some of us live there.

This happens all the time because when we are responding to something in our lives in the present or even in the future, we are reacting to every other time we've ever felt that way in our entire lives. We just aren't consciously aware of it.

This concept is part of the discussion of the Subconscious in the first chapter. Whether we identify it with the Subconscious or Critical Factor doesn't really matter. (Those concepts/categories are only to help us grasp the dynamics of what's happening, and aren't absolute or proscriptive, anyway.) Another helpful way to understand this phenomenon is through *resonance*.

A lot of us know the word from music. If a guitar and a piano are in a room together (and tuned to each other), if I strike a "G" on the piano, the G-string on the guitar will start to play, responding just to the vibrations in the air. That's *sympathetic resonance*. Of course, that has to do with the physics of vibrating air molecules in particular wavelengths that then vibrate the other G string. I can imagine most of us grasping the idea in metaphorical ways relating to our thoughts or emotions, too: "that idea resonates in me," or "that scene really resonated with me." The idea that something that happens can remind us, or make us feel deeply, or connect us with a thought or emotion, isn't new. But it is important to pause and consider the psychology of what's happening.

Our Subconscious Mind is a vast and limitless reservoir of all our experiences: memories, thoughts, sensations, reflections, lessons, information, feelings, and so on. *Everything we've ever experienced is in there*, including our reflections on those experiences, filed away with other similar or associated experiences for easy and quick retrieval. But our conscious mind isn't nearly as vast or capable.

Our conscious mind is like a laser: powerful and focused, but narrow in scope. If a laser grows too wide it becomes diffuse and loses that power. Similarly, our Conscious Mind can only hold seven to nine bits of information at a time. More than that, and it starts losing information, or becoming ineffectual. Its *power* is in its ability to *focus*.

Our mind is designed to be efficient and streamline our reactions. As we read in the previous chapter, we don't have to re-learn how to tie our shoelaces every morning, how to make breakfast or get to work. Our ancestors couldn't have survived if they had to re-learn every time whether a Saber-tooth tiger was dangerous, or a particular plant poisonous, or another human being a friend (or enemy). Our brain categorizes our experiences and lessons learned in a dizzying variety of ways, but all aimed at conserving energy, so we can focus on novel, interesting and productive new ways of being.

Resonance, in this context, is this feature of our mind in which a new experience that "feels like" or "seems like" something that is already on file in the Subconscious Mind is automatically associated with our previous experiences. All those feelings come up again, telling us what to do, how we should feel, how to react (almost always without our conscious awareness, since that would reduce the efficiency). We flinch at the incoming football. We slam on the brakes before we hit the kid running into the street. We warm to our lover's touch. We feel sick at the smell of *Amaretto*. We don't *think* about these reactions before experiencing them... and thank goodness!

This is, generally, a tremendously helpful adaptation. You can probably remember a time when this *wasn't* happening, and how awkward it was. If you're like me, knowing how to drive isn't something I think about anymore. I just *drive*. But when I was *learning* how to drive – before the programming of where to put my foot, how much pressure to apply, how far or fast to direct the steering wheel to safely turn, and so on – there was *so much* to pay attention to, it was almost overwhelming. Not to mention *dangerous*! If you have to *think* about the red lights on the car ahead of you; remember that it signals application of the brake on their part; that in an abundance of caution you should slow down also; and in order to do that you must lift your right foot off the gas pedal (keep the left foot where it is, unless you're driving a stick-shift), move the right foot six inches to the left, depress the brake pedal (but not too hard or too quickly)... by this time you've already run into the back of the leading car. Having these reactions/responses unconsciously, automatically programmed is *useful*... life-saving, at times!

But one of the downsides of this extraordinary capability is that our Subconscious Mind – all those associations, files, scripts and programs – is *difficult to change*, as we discussed in the previous chapter. Especially if we're hoping to change them with will-power alone. Will-power is, of course, a quality of the Conscious

25

Mind – a benefit of that powerful laser-like attention we can direct at things. Unfortunately, will-power, like the Conscious Mind, is limited in scope and duration. It is a finite resource. In short, we get tired and it runs out. Often much sooner than we'd like.

Have you ever tried to change a habit or belief by will-power alone? Even if you were successful, I doubt you'd describe it as an easy process. And if it worked for you, then you're one of the lucky ones.

Basically there's only three ways to change those deep, long-running scripts in the subconscious: significant traumatic experience (like the aforementioned night in college chasing that bottle of amaretto); a protracted, repeated experience; and hypnosis.

Hypnosis is able to work directly with the Subconscious and intentionally re-wire some of that programming.

Resonance dominates our lives – it touches every emotion, every habitual act, every deeply held belief, every assumption about our world, good or bad. Most powerfully, because it operates in the background, we are *very rarely consciously aware* of it. Whenever we react – especially when we *overreact* – resonance is there, strumming our heartstrings. Which is why something so seemingly trivial (in any other context) can trigger such a disproportionate response. Resonance reaches back and accesses any experience that feels like that, sounds like that, looks like that, smells like that, rhymes with that (metaphorically, and possibly literally). Our Subconscious accesses not only those previous experiences, but also our thoughts, feelings, and conclusions (assumptions, really) *about* those experiences. And this all happens in *nanoseconds* and almost entirely *out of conscious awareness* (because conscious processing would take too long – like slowing when we see brake lights).

Like the guitar responding to the piano, the vibrations of one note resonating in both instruments tuned to the same frequency, new experiences resonate with previous experiences. This is literally how we make sense of them. Without previous experiences to compare or contrast or help "sort" the new experience, the new data is maddeningly meaningless.

If you've never heard a particular language before, and then are dropped into a conversation in that language, there is *no hope* of you understanding any of it… unless you can resort to some *shared*, pre-existing symbols or experience (hand-gestures, familiar loan words, pointing at objects or motions, etc.). We automatically start looking for experiences or "knowledge" that helps us make sense of what is going on around us. This is hard-wired into how we find (or, rather, *make*) meaning. So, we struggle until we find a toehold in the new language or conversation, or whatever new circumstance or context we find ourselves in. And that toehold is precisely something we *already* know, something with which we are already familiar, a "hook" we can hang this new experience on (or box we can sort it into). We need to find some resonance. Resonance just happens, for better or worse, helpful or not, *true or false*. And this is where things get tricky.

Because whenever we encounter something "familiar," we aren't just responding to *it*. We are responding to *every other time* in our lives when we felt that way. Every other time someone looked at us that way, used that tone of voice, made us feel that way, moved that way… whatever. So instead of simply reacting to *this one person* or circumstance, we are reacting to *every* time we felt that way: every other time in our lives, for instance, when we felt belittled, or let down, or threatened, or vulnerable, or unworthy, or scared, Our Subconscious says something to the effect of: "Here we go again! I know what to do, how to respond!" And we unconsciously/unthinkingly overreact: livid, paralyzed, despondent, frustrated, crushed... whatever. All those previous experiences and feelings inform this one present circumstance, and sometimes we explode.

When we think about it in this sense, we aren't "overreacting" at all – *our response was perfectly appropriate* for a lifetime of associated anger, fear, sadness, guilt, frustration or the like. If we could peel back the layers and look at all the previous programming and experience, *of course* one would respond this way! Whether or not it was an accurate understanding of the present circumstance (the other person's tone of voice or intention, for example) doesn't really make a difference at that point. Whether or not any of the previous experiences were properly understood isn't really a consideration. Realistically, how could we expect someone to understand perfectly and objectively all their previous experiences and assumptions, many of which were made before they were even old enough to understand the world or make accurate assumptions about it. Most *adults* find it difficult sometimes to have a more objective perspective or accurate understanding about their experiences in the present!

If we had the opportunity to really understand someone, what informed them and shaped them and how they understood what was happening and how to respond appropriately... we would profoundly understand why they responded they way they did (or the way we did). It doesn't make the response "good" or even objectively "appropriate" - just understandable. And this isn't only retrospectively true.

Oftentimes, when we are worried about something in the *future*, it is really an unconscious projection of all those past experiences into an *expectation* of that future event. Our fear or foreboding isn't about that upcoming speech, confrontation, or first date at all, but really about all those feelings and experiences from our past. But we can't go back and examine the code underlying our reactions, because it is all buried in the Subconscious.

At least, not with our conscious attention alone.

One of the most powerful tools available to human minds is the ability to examine – and reprogram – that background script or code running our mental-emotional operating system. It is the foundation of all psychology, in fact: how do we access, understand, and intentionally shape the Subconscious? Because resonance is the foundational principle of how we understand *everything*, how we move through the world. The task of our lives is to tune our heartstrings the way we *want*, rather than however our heartstrings happened to have been tuned by experiences we didn't understand and assumptions we haven't had the power to reconsider.

Will-power alone is all-too-often insufficient to effect real change in our lives. At best, we might create a new response or reaction through the brute force of "classical conditioning," but this leaves the fundamental (mistaken/inaccurate/unhelpful) programming in place. Or does it…?

Let us explore the dynamics of resonance a little more by diving into a specific feeling: fear.

Chapter 3
How Fear is Like Flypaper

In 1920, psychologist John Watson and his graduate student Rosalie Rayner conducted an ethically questionable experiment on conditioning fear. An 11 month-old child was exposed to various animals and showed no natural signs of fear or concern. Through the course of the experiment, the child, referred to as "Little Albert,"was startled by a loud clang – a hammer hitting a steel pipe behind him – every time he was also exposed to a white rat. It didn't take long before Little Albert was sensitized or conditioned to be upset by the sight of the white rat, even without the original and naturally upsetting clang. Albert was essentially intentionally programmed with a fear of the white rat.

Albert's fear quickly generalized to *other* animals (a white rabbit, then the family dog), cotton wool, and even a man's white beard. It was a demonstration of how fears and anxiety can generalize beyond their original associations or conditioning. Albert's fear was like fly-paper, sticking to whatever came near it, catching all sorts of unnecessary and unhelpful associations. You can imagine a fly-paper anxiety quickly becoming quite a mess. Other experiments since Little Albert, more ethical and under stricter protocols, have continued to demonstrate how anxieties and fears can generalize, and this has become a pillar of classical conditioning, behaviorism, and elementary psychology. This probably seems reasonable, and proven by our own everyday lives and experience. What is important to highlight, however, is that it demonstrates that the *original* source of anxiety/fear/phobia/response isn't necessarily, explicitly the same thing as the *presenting* problem.

This makes sense for most people intellectually. It is important for people who are dealing with anxieties or fears understand this important point. Sometimes what they *think* is the problem, even what they are *experiencing* as the problem, might not be the *source* of the problem. This is why work in hypnosis can be so powerful. In hypnosis, we are bypassing (to a degree) the "logic" and structure of the Conscious Mind – that part that wants things to "make sense," be linear, show a line of cause-and-effect, be obviously related. The Conscious Mind is a great editor, striking out things that don't (seem to) make sense or what it perceives to be "mistakes." And, of course, the Conscious Mind can only focus on so much (not very much at all) – it is like a laser, really powerful when focused but pretty useless when diffused.

The problem is that the Subconscious Mind isn't organized "logically" (at least a logic that the Conscious Mind would recognize). The Subconscious is organized by *association* – what feels the same, smells the same, sounds the same, looks to require a similar response or reaction, and so on – which is a much more efficient way of dealing with millions of bits of information. How these associations are created, strengthened, or changed is oftentimes a matter of chance in childhood and early development. Remember, there is no *objective* knowledge in the Subconscious Mind; it is all *subjective* knowledge, what we happened to have experienced and what we happen to have thought about those experiences. So sometimes we make some pretty surprising connections.

When in conscious conversation or reflection, we might (even pre-consciously or unconsciously) edit out associations that "don't make sense." So our conscious reflections or memories or assumptions might not be working with all the information, particularly the *deepest* or *earliest* information (that is more likely to "not make sense" since we processed those experiences long before we had any extended knowledge about how the world works). So it can't *change* those deepest or earliest assumptions/associations. But *in deep hypnosis*, guided by a skilled and ethical hypnotist, we are often able to highlight and explore those earlier experiences, and even revise the mistaken beliefs we had as a result of them.

There are, predictably, more approaches than this type of regression. Another approach rests in the behavioral camp and seeks to address the issue exclusively by focusing on *behaviors* around the presenting issue. The logic rests on the relationship between what we *do* and who we *are*. For Behaviorists, those two are practically the same – our behaviors stem from our "beliefs" (internal programming), so if we can change the behaviors it will reciprocally reprogram the underlying beliefs. This school of thought caught fire in the early 20th century, led by the pioneering Soviet researcher Ivan Pavlov, and adapted by American psychologists like B.F. Skinner. One great advantage to this approach is the obvious ability to measure results in physical experiments: how does the behavior change? If we are simply mobile computers spitting out programmed responses, then once the responses have changed, the programming has necessarily changed, too. Even outside this rather stark appraisal of human capacity, most people come to hypnosis (and to psychologists and counselors) to change *what they are doing*. If it is the goal to stop smoking, biting nails, gambling, or being afraid of snakes, then once we have conditioned that behavior away, we have been successful! There is no need to look for "what caused" the problem behavior – just *change the behavior*.

Early-20th century behavioral clinical psychologist, Andrew Salter objected to "regression to cause" with the reasoning that *identification of the original source* or context of the conditioning *is not sufficient* for re-programming. He used the colorful example that a patient is not healed by knowing whether the freight that ran him over was headed north or south. This is true, of course, and is also representative of Salter's acerbic and entertaining rhetorical style. But it also oversimplifies and thus easily dismisses the real work (and power) of age regression. To the contrary, Salter inadvertently emphasizes the important point that merely *identifying* the source is not sufficient. *Insight* must be brought to bear. That is, new and sufficiently transformative understanding that changes the underlying assumptions about the original context or conditioning. Insight (in this sense) is itself re-conditioning, or even *un*-conditioning, the original source associations, effectively un-linking them and undoing the complex that led to the expanded/generalized fear or reaction the individual is experiencing now.

Again, simply *identifying* the source or original conditioning/association isn't enough for transformative change. One must help the client use the client's best understanding (their current, mature, more-informed knowledge) to change the context or conditioning. Hypnosis help their younger self be able to experience those instances without the need to make the unnecessary, unhelpful or mistaken associations that were made originally out of ignorance. This frees the younger self from the original associations, effectively stopping the chain of generalized fears from forming.

It is then important that the individual witness the ramifications of this change, by walking through their successive experiences and associations (the fearful circumstances or situations) in order to fully grasp this far-reaching chain of generalization. This is a sophisticated and nuanced variety of "parts work": having the "adult part" coach the "younger part" through an experience, knowing what the adult part knows now. Then the younger part walks through successive experiences, seeing the cascading change rippling through the years, freeing the younger part(s) from those unnecessary and unhelpful associations.

I do this with my clients every day in formal hypnosis sessions. But this is also something I want them to be able to do even after our sessions have concluded. It is something I have my children do. It is a technique I regularly use on myself – in self-hypnosis and sometimes just watering the garden. I have a deliberate, compassionate conversation with my earlier self, to let him know what is going to happen (I can't change history, or other people's actions), and what is *really* going on. I tell him it probably isn't about him at all, or likely not as much as he thought; the other people are reacting to their own issues; it isn't his fault; he is loveable and good; anyone who experienced what he experienced would feel the same way, and so on. I make sure those beliefs and understandings of my younger self are informed by my best understanding *now*, as an adult with more experience and awareness of other people and how the world works. Most of our fears are based on incorrect understandings or beliefs – and no wonder! We are responding to programs that were installed in us years before we could have known what was really going on! Given what we had experienced (at that moment and also earlier, leading up to that experience, shaping our beliefs and assumptions and our sense of an appropriate response), *of course* we responded that way! "Now, little me, let me tell you what's really going on, and how smart, good, loveable, worthy (and so on) you are."

Then the little me walks through that experience again, knowing what I do now, with a more objective, mature, compassionate, knowing perspective.

It is magical. For my clients, for my kids, for me.

Most people, I believe, can imaginatively grasp this idea quite readily: instead of having to uproot an entire forest, you can simply go back and un-plant that first seed, and then walk through time to see how that landscape looks without the crowded roots and thickets.

With this powerful reprogramming of our immediate, unconscious beliefs/assumptions/reactions – whether we call it "hypnosis" or "active imagination" or even "lucid dreaming" – the real proof is in the pudding, as they say: have we *changed* how we respond in that troublesome situation?

Andrew Salter, that abrasive and entertaining critic of the "regression-to-cause" approach I mentioned earlier, took the litmus test of *results* so seriously he based his entire practice and theory on it. He noticed in studies of people who were successful in therapy (meaning they changed what they wanted to change) that they tended to report feeling more assertive and self-sufficient. They reported being more bold and having healthier personal boundaries, regardless of what the particular issue they came to therapy to address. He turned the therapy on its head and asked: if, when people feel better, they report feeling more assertive, then why not just help people be more assertive. Salter wrote that he believed everyone came to his practice with fundamentally the same problem, so everyone got fundamentally the same treatment: assertiveness training. (Salter called it being "excitatory," but I don't think that term gained currency, even among fans of his work. So I'll just call it "assertiveness.")

I think Salter's work has a lot to recommend it. Most importantly, it reminds us of the importance of instilling both coping mechanisms (including alternative behaviors and reactions) *and* confidence that the client can handle the situation (self-efficacy, self-reliance). Whether or not the assertiveness itself "solves the issue," it certainly helps build confidence that we *can* make different choices, have different reactions, have more control over ourselves and the direction of our lives. And despite his protests, Salter's approach reminds us that the "presenting problem" might be rooted in something seemingly unrelated. Marriage problems, kleptomania, insomnia, irritable bowel syndrome… for Salter they were all rooted in too much personal inhibition. We don't have to agree with what he identifies as the "real" cause of issues to appreciate the fundamental point: what we experience as a problem in our lives is a problem, but it might not be where the problem started, or fundamentally what needs to be addressed to experience lasting change.

Not too long ago, I helped a friend move her washing machine a few feet. Not a big deal, I thought. But the next day and for the following week, I had a persistent and disturbing pain at the base of my neck. So I went to see a massage therapist. As I lay on the table, she seemed to be working all *around* the problem, but not at it. She went pretty far afield: my back, my deltoids, my pectorals, trapezius, even behind my ears, and so on. She hardly even touched where I felt the pain at the base of my neck. Don't get me wrong, it was heavenly. I loved it. But it wasn't addressing the issue I went in for. Except…

When I rose from the table, and reached to put on my shirt, there was no pain. My range of motion had returned. I felt so much better – physically, mentally, even emotionally. It was incredible. And I gladly paid her double what she asked for.

Sometimes we need to trust the experts, even when they aren't doing what we would expect them to be doing. *They* might know what they are doing. In this case, the therapist knew the surrounding issues that were contributing to or causing my discomfort – so just rubbing the spot where it hurt wouldn't have helped, or helped much. She needed to address the underlying and contributing causes, and once that was done, wouldn't you know it, the "problem" was easy to solve, the pain easy to let go of. And I rose from her table a new man.

It sometimes happens that a client of mine will be surprised at what comes up in our work, or by what I choose to focus on in a given session, observing intellectually that it doesn't clearly relate to or seem to be "the source" of the problem or issue they came in for help with. There might be an implicit question, or even be bordering on a complaint.

I had a client that had come in for fear of riding bicycles – he recently developed the fear, even though he loves riding bikes. As we traced the roots of the feelings he was experiencing, we went all over his childhood and young adulthood. He came back the next session and commented that we weren't dealing with what he was paying me to work on... and he wasn't even in hypnosis, by the way. Despite all that, immediately afterwards he nonchalantly comments on how much he's been enjoying riding his bike lately, not having any issues. (He didn't even see the connection!) Sometimes it doesn't "make sense" from the outside, but the real answer is in the relief and change.

It seems to me that hypnosis might find a helpful analogy in massage therapy. The felt problem, or presenting issue, or change needed, might be the "pinch point" for lack of a better term, but it might not be the *source* of the problem. We may need to address the surrounding emotional musculature, if you will, the pull of different muscles in different (even distant) parts of the mental body. It may be that a seemingly unrelated behavior – posture, compensation, gait, favoring one side to another, and so on – may be contributing to the issue. It might be tension in another part of one's self is being "felt" in *this* area of one's life. If I simply offer direct suggestion to alleviate the suffering, the discomfort may depart for a while, but the behaviors, postures, or tensions that caused it will still be there to cause it again.

In my own practice, I trust the Subconscious to know what the real issue is, and to guide us in addressing what needs to be addressed. I am explicitly open to tracing the problem *feeling* to earlier experiences or assumptions/ beliefs that might "appear" to be distantly related or even unrelated altogether. The Conscious Mind, as I pointed out earlier, is logical, causal, linear. The Subconscious isn't limited by those restrictions, being loosely organized by association, expressed oftentimes by feelings. Those feelings, therefore, provide a link or stepping stone to underlying associations (experiences and beliefs), which "on the surface" (that is, to the Conscious Mind) may seem wholly unrelated. The litmus test for successful hypnosis is not whether the association/experience/belief/ memory appears logically or causally determinative of the problem, but whether the client experiences positive change. If the client is experiencing the benefit – relief, comfort, empowerment, freedom, whatever – then we are doing the work that needs to be done. I'm pressing the right points, releasing the right tension, despite the appearance of it being distant or not of obvious relevance.

Reflecting on my massage experience, I recall at times the therapist would be pressing on one spot on my body, and I would "feel" it (or something related to it?) in another part of my body. She pressed on a knot in the middle of my back, and my right arm was palpably warm. Or my middle finger would twitch when she massaged the base of my skull. She called it a "referral" - which must be massage therapist talk for what I would describe as an associated somatic reaction. (Admittedly, "referral" is easier to say.)

This phenomenon is similar to the one observed above, in the sense that it is the same process just backwards. Somatically, in the body, the tension (or relief) in one place is "felt" in another place, perhaps in a different way altogether. It is a demonstration of the association of *seemingly* unrelated phenomena in meaningful and informative ways. I've often heard stories of people on the massage table feeling flooded with an emotion and breaking into tears as a certain muscle is massaged, for instance. Just as I felt in my arm the work the therapist was doing on my back, my clients might feel in their present difficulty the benefit of releasing misunderstandings stemming from an early-childhood experience (for example), or freedom from smoking by letting go of their anger at significant others who have hurt them.

If someone is constantly questioning the relevance of what the professional is doing, they will not be able to relax and feel the benefit of the work – either massage or hypnosis. The real proof of expertise is, in the end, does it work? Is there change? Does the client *feel better* in lasting and meaningful ways? In hypnosis, just as in massage, it is best to just relax and enjoy the process – whatever it is – trusting the professional to know what they are doing and that new freedom of movement awaits us at the end.

These insights and understanding hold fundamentally good news: Yes, fear can be generalized, it can be like fly-paper collecting and affecting so much.

But so can *healing*. We may be in for a surprising journey of profound transformation, liberation, and empowerment. We may rise from the experience a new person.

What would it feel like, not just to be free from what holds us back, but to have never been held back by it at all? That is the question I start with, and the one the client ends up answering for themselves.

Chapter 4
Foreign Language Learning and Social Ho]
The Hidden (Hypnotic) Value of Learn....
Another Language

I was invited to speak at an international philology and psycholinguistics conference in southern Ukraine in early 2020, because of my experience there teaching English as a foreign language (in the early 2000s) and my current work in hypnosis. The conference took place, obviously, before the 2022 Russian escalation/invasion in Ukraine, which made the somewhat-theoretical or abstractly-removed predictions I raised in the paper even more prescient in hindsight. What follows reflects the political situation in 2020: Russia has already occupied and illegally "annexed" Crimea, and was orchestrating and supplying a war in Ukraine's eastern region under the thin veneer of local independence movements. The unexpectedly effective Ukrainian resistance to the Russian invasion makes some of the remaining observations about Ukraine in the following pages even more relevant.

The theme of the conference focused on the dynamics of education in the multi-ethnic *Budzhak* region. The *Budzhak* region is made up largely of a dogleg of Ukraine that extends south along The Black Sea, bordering Romania in the south and Moldova in the west, between the Dniester and Danube rivers. This sparsely populated and somewhat-isolated area has for centuries been on the edges of larger empires, from Romans to Mongols, Ottomans to Russians, Soviets to the European Union. The etymology of the name *Budzhak* (also spelled *Budjak*) itself lies in the Ottoman word for "borderland," which echoes the same Slavic origin of "Ukraine."

Something about this region speaks deeply to being both out-of-the-way and somehow vitally important.

As is often the case, these liminal spaces are sites of mixing, fluidity, and sometimes friction. The Polish-American political scientist Zbigniew Brzezinski spoke of geopolitical "pivot points" - areas that were valuable to larger powers not particularly because of some intrinsic quality but because of the resources or geography that area provides access to. The *Budjak* is just such a potential geopolitical hot-spot, with its proximity and land-access to Moldova and Romania. Russian-supported breakaway movements and ethnic divisions already destabilize Moldova along its borders with Ukraine, and the oil-rich Romanian region just south of the Danube would be a tempting resource for any expanding empire to secure.

Importantly, the *Budjak* is ethnically diverse, with Russians, Ukrainians, Romanians, Bulgarians, and Gagauz, among many others, living in relatively separate, silo-ed communities. With deep historical, cultural, and religious differences, it is fertile soil for the seeds of Russian propaganda fomenting division along ethnic and linguistic lines.

The largest city and administrative center, Izmail, hosts a pedagogical university that teaches, among other things, foreign language education. It is my contention that learning a foreign language, at least initially, requires and facilitates hypnotic phenomena. At the same it time also uniquely prepares learners-as-adults to better resist divisive propaganda and instead see the value and integrity of the stranger/foreigner/Other. Basically, learning another language makes one a better neighbor.

In order to learn a foreign language, one must create a new space in one's mind – a kind of provisional, temporary intellectual space, where the rules one has already learned don't apply, but where one is confident that things will make sense, even if at first they seem nonsensical. Encountering strange words, new sounds and phonemes, different grammar and patterns and exceptions, oftentimes a completely different alphabet, all contribute to this necessity for a quasi-dissociated state that is still somehow integral. That is, a mental space that is at once "other" than one's self *and* a part of oneself, both foreign and familiar, strange and somehow already beloved. The shock and novelty of learning a foreign language both induces and requires a dissociated state (for lack of a better term) where one starts with the assumption that what one has heretofore known as the sole "truth" (a native language or "mother tongue") is but *one* truth, one possibility among many valid possibilities, and that something even wildly *different* can be *true* as well. It can hold beauty and meaning and utility, even joy.

This also occurs, of course, when deeply learning any new system: mathematics, chemistry, music, philosophy, poetry, international politics, chess, and so on. We create a mental (and sometimes emotional) structure where these new learnings are held as provisionally-true, confident that we will at some point be able to understand them on their own terms. When learning chess, for example, the knight moves in an "L" shape – an easy association even if the "L" is backwards or upside-down. The Bishop moves diagonally and the Queen moves freely in any direction. Why can't the Bishop step forward? No idea. It doesn't make sense. That's just the way it is. Eventually, we are able to just accept the new structure and see the beauty and interior logic of the game, and even transcend the "L" image altogether to simply move the knight, not needing to question.

45

With foreign language, however, there is the added, unique component of *interpersonal meaning*: of culture and value, of worth and reason. Foreign language study starts with the assumption that there is something valuable in what *people* who are different from us are doing, how they think, how they construct and convey meaning and importance. To learn a different language we must start with a kind of love, an expectancy, an interest and focus, a care. We must have, on some level, an intent to not only appreciate the unfamiliar but deepen our appreciation: we must believe there is truth and worth in this strange, new world.

This requires a state of mind open to the likelihood of the stranger, the foreigner, the Other, the Different. It requires a perspective that is both different *and* true, both not-the-same-as-mine *and* legitimate; concerns and ways of constructing meaning that might seem nonsensical to "us" but that can at the same time be integral, reasonable, and meaningful to "them." There is value in learning how to understand and engage in their worldview, learning how to swim in *their* sea, if you will.

This predisposition to see the good and the true and the valuable in the stranger is, perhaps, the greatest unspoken lesson of foreign language learning. It is presumed and nourished. Teachers know deeply the power of joy in creating and sustaining interest on the part of students. If students can make *emotional* connections, particularly positive ones at first, they learn faster, incorporate the information more deeply, and are more resilient when making mistakes. If students can have fun and enjoy the process of learning a new language, they are far more predisposed to do the hard mental work it takes, and even to not see the effort as "hard" or "work" at all. Foreign language teachers may not realize it consciously, of course, but they are teaching *love* first: interest, care, attentiveness, curiosity, assuming the best (that the Other makes sense, that that sense is worth hearing), assuming good intentions (those other-language-speakers are not trying to deceive us or make fun of us). This positive predisposition is fundamental to learning a new language.

One quality required (and induced by) learning a foreign language, is an *increased openness to suggestion*, a receptivity to new conditioning. That is the definition of hypnosis, and is the product of a temporarily semi-dissociated state that is seeking to make sense of the seemingly non-sensical. Acceptance of this receptive mind-set is essential for learning a language beyond rote memorization or simple word-substitution. This "openness to suggestion" is what we have been describing above, as required by deep learning of any new system of meaning. In acquiring a new language, however, the suggestions of grammar, vocabulary, structure and meaning, are underlain by a fundamental, almost unconscious affirmation of the *value* of the Other, and the student's ability to apprehend (if with some effort) the perspective of the Other. The learners, at best, don't simply see the target language "from the outside," as it were, but work to previvify their own lives in that new milieu with confidence and fluency. This is even more the case with the opportunity to learn with a native speaker of the target language (as has been the case for many years at Izmail State University of the Humanities, who have recruited Germans and Americans for decades to work as foreign language faculty).

Studying foreign languages and culture, especially with a native speaker educator, creates a novel intellectual space that disorientates the mind and opens up the possibility for deep changes in attitudes and exposure to new ideas, people, populations, values, and traditions. Dissociation is a phenomenon that cannot be entirely compartmentalized – it can affect mental "programming" not under direct examination or attention, like prejudices and assumptions about the motives or value of other individuals or communities. This has profound implications for adult education in multi-ethnic communities, particularly in regions where ethnic strife and division might be mobilized to foment disruption by a foreign interest. Foreign language exposure – of any foreign language – in helping students appreciate the value and perspective of strangers, can help build resilience in adults against propaganda and attempts to alienate neighbors and neighboring ethnic communities. Learning to love a foreign language as students helps us love foreign *people* as adults.

The *Budzhak* region is one of tremendous ethnic and linguistic diversity, but also a region where these different communities are still largely "silo-ed" or geographically isolated from each other. Geographically isolated from the rest of Ukraine as a whole, and bordering several locations of political strife in Moldova, the *Budzhak* poses a particularly sensitive and important object lesson in the value of being able to listen to people and communities different from one's own. The *Budzhak* is geopolitically valuable to interfering nations because of its proximity to these areas of conflict and its access to the Black Sea. If *Budzhak* is, as Zbigniew Brzezinski put it, a geopolitical "pivot point," and Russia foments division in Ukraine and Moldova as ethnic "independence" or breakaway movements as a way to destabilize near-neighbors and possibly provide a pretext for invasion/occupation by Russian forces or interests, then Izmail State University's yearly churning out of informed, educated, and open-minded graduates may be among the greatest stabilizing assets in that region.

Propaganda itself could be considered a kind of dissociated state (in a negative and manipulative sense, hypnosis) that creates a context where people are open to certain kinds of suggestions and conditioning, specifically the idea that one's "foreign" neighbors do not share the same interests as oneself, or are at worst opposed to one's own desire for a peaceful, productive, secure life. Education, therefore, is not a unique use of conditioning, but actually an *antidote* to broader manipulation. It is in effect *un-hypnotizing* individuals from intellectual or ethnic silos. Where powers or principalities would manipulate us into seeing the worst in our neighbors, sowing distrust and division, foreign language instruction fosters a profound resilience against the simplistic and irrational claims of nationalism or ethnic division.

This is the same psycho-emotional phenomenon that makes storytelling such a powerful political tool: it makes an emotional connection and we begin to identify with the storyteller, to absorb or appreciate their perspective (even as our own). This was the primary strategy that is responsible for the shift in our culture around LGBTQ rights in the past 30 years: there was a deliberate effort to tell their stories as people, their lives and struggles and identities. Most of us straight folk heard our own experiences echoed in those stories, and we understood more, sympathized more, identified *with* more. It wasn't reasoned arguments or logical postulates that changed people's hearts and minds. We straight folk weren't forced by reason or violence to accept the full humanity of our gay and lesbian brothers and sisters. It was our growing understanding of, and identification with them that erased the lines our prejudice and previous programming had drawn.

Now, the transgender community is riding the proverbial coat-tails of this cultural shift, leaning into our collective openness of heart and mind, and telling their stories. What took the lesbian and gay community two generations to accomplish, the transgender community is achieving in a decade or two: we are hearing their stories and feeling them increasingly as part of our own. For some of us (particularly younger generations) it may barely have registered on our radar, it seemed such a natural extension of who we are as a civilization. Our openness to sympathizing with and including "others" in "us" can seem the most natural thing in the world.

* * *

In the Russian language there is a subtle and curious phenomenon. While in Ukraine as a Peace Corps Volunteer from 1999 to 2002, I lived and worked primarily in the *Budzhak* region. There were so many languages present there, that Peace Corps thought it best if I learn Russian, effectively the market language, so I could communicate with most everyone. I was the only native English speaker within a five-hour bus ride, so when I made friends we spoke primarily Russian together. At first, I was a stranger – a welcome stranger and an object of curiosity, but a stranger nonetheless. When I was introduced to new people or communities it often felt a little like I was on exhibit.

At some unknown point, however – perhaps I had been there long enough, or my language skills were strong enough, or I simply shared enough experiences with the people around me – at some point things felt different. I was no longer one of "them." I was part of an "us." And when I was introduced to new people or groups, I was introduced as *nash* – not "our volunteer," or "our friend," just "*ours.*" "It's ok," they'd sometimes say, "he's *ours.*" In Russian, this possessive pronoun when applied to people has a different connotation than it might have in English. It means something closer to "one of us." It implies a level of familiarity, trust, and inclusion one has reached to be described as *nash.*

It wasn't any logic or argument that drew me into their circle. People already knew a lot about Americans, and Ukrainians are reasonable people who understand there are good people and bad in every civilization. It was shared experience, care, *love* that included me in their sphere of identity. We were given the opportunity, created in part by the novelty of our situation (an *American* living in little *Izmail*?!), to reprogram subconscious/unconscious prejudices and divisions, to see each other as extensions of ourselves, as holding the same worth and value and complexity and dignity and fun as ourselves. I was *nash.*

This sort of thing happens all the time, in many different ways – it is what *learning* is all about: reprogramming our expectations about ourselves and the world. The novelty of a foreign language dissociates the mind by forcing the creation of temporary considerations of new/novel data. We hypnotize ourselves to learn a new language. This is *how* we learn languages. But it also fosters a fundamental openness that can also be mobilized for implicit (and explicit) cross-cultural diversity training, lifting up the value and dignity of other populations, traditions, ethnicities, and perspectives (worldviews, political interests, etc.). It opens the possibility for profound programming at a subconscious level, orientating students to be adults predisposed to assume value and integrity in the perspectives and interests of other/different cultures, and less likely to give credence to divisive and alienating propaganda. In short, learning a foreign language makes for more understanding, more generous, more respectful and resilient neighbors. That is important in the *Budzhak*, and it is an important lesson for everyone, everywhere.

This isn't just about languages, of course. This is what happens when we deeply learn anything. Learning requires or creates a kind of hypnosis (hypnosis *is* learning), and that can be taken advantage of for propaganda purposes to drive people away from each other, to mistrust each other. Or it can open up the opportunity for people to create new connections, affiliations, and sympathies with people they might have earlier considered complete "strangers." There are many ways to help innoculate people against propaganda, bigotry, divisiveness, or prejudice, but one of the most surprising might be something not explicitly related to "diversity training" at all: learning a foreign language. Learning another language lays down an intellectual and emotional framework for shared meaning and value, especially when it is "different" than one's own. Learning to speak to another heart in their own langauge opens up one's own heart as well. That is the hidden value in learning a foreign language.

Chapter 5
Transformation Trance Formation

Our minds are incredible, layered, complex… and can both hamstring us into repeating old patterns or open us up to profound and meaningful change. Let's opt for the latter, and take more control of the unconscious forces guiding our lives.

Here is a simple technique of self-hypnosis – not necessarily unique to me. It is a simplified version of what I teach my own clients, in fact. So it is grounded in both the theory and practice I work with every day.

There are basically three parts that are repeated for as long as you want to do the practice – as little as 5 minutes, as much as 20 minutes, or even an hour to two, if you like. It starts with a well-formulated suggestion, then involves two instances of active imagination or fantasizing. Then returns to the suggestion, and continues again.

Let us walk through these in a little more detail.

Step One – A Well-Formulated Suggestion

Hypnosis is all about *suggestions*. "Suggestion" is just what hypnotists call statements, ideas, concepts, feelings, that we *want* the client to adopt. Some of these can be overt, some covertly made (hidden in the context of other statements designed to distract the Conscious Mind from resisting the suggestion). Oftentimes the best suggestions are the ones the client makes themselves.

There are some helpful guidelines for what makes suggestions more effective or easier for the Subconscious to accept. First, it should be **phrased in the *positive***. I don't mean that it should be "optimistic" or even worse "polyannish." I mean grammatically positive.

The Subconscious has difficulty recognizing *negatives*. It simply sees the topic, the *thing*, whether it is "supposed" to think of that thing or not. If I told you to *not* think of a pink elephant... of course you think of a pink elephant, and then weirdly try to force it from your mind. You probably hadn't thought of pink elephants for years, and yet here you are, having been told not to think of them and they come repeatedly to mind. (Stop saying "pink elephants!")

If I really didn't want you to think of a pink elephant, almost the worst thing I could do would be to tell you not to think of one. It would be much more effective if I told you to think of something else altogether: a red fox, or your first kiss, or the last movie you saw.

When I am working with clients, trying to specify what it is they actually want to achieve, oftentimes the first place they go is to what they *don't* want to experience any more: smoking, stress, anger, fear, low-self-esteem... whatever. We're really good at identifying what we *don't* want. It is good to know what you don't want! But it is also important to know what you *do* want, and *that* makes a good suggestion.

The best suggestions aren't negative (identifying what you *don't* want), but positive (identifying what you *do* want).

Good suggestions should also be ***achievable* or *realistic***. Wanting to fly isn't a great suggestion because, well, without some additional apparatus, it isn't realistic. There is, of course, a lot of wiggle room here, and what for one person is impossible for another person might be a perfectly reasonable goal. Bowling above 250, for example. The key here is that the best suggestions point to something you *know* you can achieve. Stop smoking, for example. Speak comfortably in public, maybe. Handle a snake, do the splits, stand up to your boss or your boyfriend... whatever. **Don't get bogged down in *how* you're going to achieve it yet.** You don't need a roadmap or detailed plan in place to know what is realistic, if perhaps a bit hopeful. (If anything, err on the side of boldness! **Choose brave over perfect.**)

You want your suggestion to *motivate* your Subconscious to achieve your goals, not de-motivate it by suggesting something impossible, making it easy to toss the idea aside. If you can break a larger goal into smaller steps, try that. Instead of losing 300 pounds, lose 20. Better yet, don't tie the suggestion to weight at all, but to healthy, sustainable patterns like eating only as much as your body needs to function, eating lean and healthy, having more energy and exercising more, and so on.

Good suggestions have some ***measurability*** to them. We know when we've achieved them... or not. "Feeling better" is kind of ambiguous. "Climbing Mt. Rainier" is definite – either I have or haven't. If you are coming at this task with something along the "feeling better" lines, ask yourself how would you know if you are feeling better. What difference would it make in your life? How would your life look different? And measure *that*.

If I felt better, I might play more Ultimate Frisbee in the park. So, one suggestion would focus on me playing Frisbee in the park two days a week. (Notice the quantity, there – measurable!) I would walk my dog an hour every evening. I would make love with my wife twice a week. I would spend 30 minutes every morning writing a book. Whatever "feeling better" actually looks like – do that.

Get measurable!

Good suggestions take place in the **present**. "Tomorrow" is the enemy of success, when phrasing suggestions for our Subconscious. The future tense is never-ending, so your goal could never happen and it would *still* be true in the Subconscious – because there is still future out there. (Until you're dead. But at that point the effectiveness of your hypnotic suggestions is a moot point.) Form the suggestion as if you have already achieved it.

I know this seems strange to the Conscious Mind - "but I *haven't* yet" it whines, killing motivation with "logic." Shut up, Conscious Mind.

Point is, phrase your suggestions to be in the present, right *now*. I *am* 20 lbs healthier. I *am* bowling above 250. I *am* spending time listening to my kids. I *am* more energetic. I *am* climbing Mt. Rainier. Je *suis* parle Francais. I *am* speaking articulately to my team. Whatever it is – make it *now*. Why wait to be a badass?

So, to summarize, well-formulated suggestions are positive, achievable, measurable, and in the present (as if you've already achieved them). Create a well-crafted suggestion for what you want to achieve or change. It should be short, easy to remember, and to the point.

Also, it shouldn't be *too* specific. We don't want to shackle our imagination to unnecessary details, like "I am climbing Mt. Rainier on Tuesday, August 1, 2023, summiting at 3:44am with my red parka and my yellow gloves on, looking southwest and eating a chocolate chip peanut butter granola bar." We want wiggle room. You'll see why in the next step.

This step is simple and straightforward. Get yourself into a comfortable position where you can safely close your eyes for a few minutes. Then begin with simply saying your well-crafted suggestion to yourself (in your mind). Then, insert a fantasy of you achieving the goal or making the change you desire.

Step Two – A Fantasy Achieving the Goal or Making the Change You Desire
I say "fantasy" and not "visualization" because when we visualize we see ourselves as if from the outside, in the third-person, witnessing ourselves do the thing. Visualization is a powerful tool for programming expectations, but even more powerful than visualization is *fantasy*. When we fantasize, we experience the event or action in the first-person, "from the inside." In a way, we are pre-living that event. Fantasy is even more powerful in programming the Subconscious for a number of reasons.

First, good fantasies are *specific*, rather than general. In the same way that good compliments are. If I told you that you dressed well… well, that's nice, probably feels good, thank you very much. But what if I told you: You know that blazer you wore to your presentation to the team last week, that was just perfect for that occasion. It expressed professionalism and leadership, but also approachability and collegiality. It showed that you took your role seriously and had prepared, but that you were really interested in having us all contribute. And the colors of the blazer, I noticed, even subtly matched the campaign we're working on. Well done." Now *that* compliment is specific, it is sharper, it goes in deeper and makes more of an impact in the Subconscious Mind.

Similarly, specific fantasies have more of an impact. You've probably noticed this yourself, that a good fantasy seems to zero in on some quality, facet, or action, and can replay it or slow it down or focus on multiple, different qualities or details, making it more rich, textured, vibrant. Sometimes it feels more real than reality!

Fantasies are so profoundly impactful in part because of this quality of *feeling real* at the same time as being able to bend the normal rules of reality. They allow us to focus on important or pleasurable details, perhaps more so than when living through a moment (that passes quickly and is full of potential distractions and other concerns). To intentionally fantasize, really **dial down on one, two, or at most three qualities/details of that change that you want to make**, or the goal you want to achieve.

Don't try to cram in all aspects of that change or goal into one fantasy. Don't feel rushed or pressured to get it *right* or to get it *all*. Over the course of this practice, you can have as many different fantasies as you like. So spend each one diving deep into just one or two aspects of that change, that new experience you are living into. You can do this as many times as you like, as many different ways as you like. The main key is for you to really *get into* the fantasy.

Holding the bowling ball the perfect way. Twisting the golf swing exactly right. Speaking a few really good lines perfectly, then continuing on with other information, knowing that information and your articulateness is ringing in your audience's head and taking them on a mini-emotional-journey. Meanwhile you continue, smiling to yourself, knowing you nailed it and it looks like this is the way it happens all the time. Capturing a spider, first under a glass, then maybe a napkin, then maybe with bare hands – quickly, confidently – and taking it outdoors to be released. Making love with your partner, rising to their touch and scent, feeling aroused and connected and focused as long and as powerfully as you need to be.

Experiencing contractions and giving birth comfortably, calmly, eagerly – feeling the universe push with/through you to hug your baby into the world. Camping outdoors, hearing the sounds of unseen critters in the dark, knowing they are not interested in you (you put the food away in the car), and able to lean back and enjoy the fascination of a sky impossibly rich with stars. Feeling the familiar fatigue and burn at mile 11 of the marathon, and running still, footstep after footstep, knowing what it is, who you are, that you've done this before, and that you've got this. Sitting an exam inexplicably confident, knowing you've studied well, that you will do well, and that whatever grade it ends up being is simply meant to help guide future studies, isn't any measure of your worth, and that you will turn the paper in with a smile, still feeling confident and pleased.

Whatever the fantasy is for you, whatever the ultimate goal is for you, try to dial in to just one or two details or facets of that experience – and really *experience* them, as deeply and richly as possible. You can have the exact same fantasy over again later, if you like, and focus on the *next* detail, or the placement of your middle finger instead of your index finger this time, for example.

You've probably heard the proverb "a picture is worth a thousand words." That's true with the Subconscious, as well. Pictures and images are more powerful than just words. But even *more* powerful than pictures are *feelings*. A feeling is worth a thousand pictures.

The more you can really bring up the feeling of achieving that goal, making that change, or living that new reality, the more impactful, meaningful, and deeply programming the fantasy will be for the Subconscious.

Feel the oneness with the bowling ball in your hand, the movement and balance and poise, as you release it perfectly. *Feel* confident, speaking to an audience fluently, articulately, meaningfully, guiding them like a puppeteer on an emotional or intellectual journey. *Feel* love of your partner and the thrill of the perfect moment as you ask them to marry you, and they accept. *Feel* the lightness and exactitude of the toe-point in the ballet performance. *Feel* the relief from chronic discomfort as you are able to do the things you want to do despite any remaining discomfort.

The more you can genuinely *feel the feelings* – the emotions, the physical sensations, the movement and pulse within you – the deeper into the fantasy you go, and the more powerful the fantasy becomes. You are literally pre-living an experience, so at a deep and unconscious level you *know* you can do it, because you *already have*. On a neurological level, you are establishing, exercising, and deepening those connections (the actions, the responses, the emotions, the understandings), empowering them to be more automatic, easier to generate and lean into and rely on. You are creating new habits, new programming out of thin air – out of nothing more than your creative imagination.

Which leads me to the third quality of good fantasies….

Good fantasies are fun! This should be the most fun you have all day, because you are living the dream! Accomplishing what you most want to accomplish, being who you most want to be, loving living every second of it! You know you are doing this practice correctly if you end it with a smile a mile wide.

Having fun is deeply programming to the Subconscious Mind. Fun opens up the mind to new programming, novel perspective, new motions and emotions, new movements and behaviors, new reactions and responses. It is why *play* is so important for young children – in many ways they are rehearsing (or *pre*hearsing?) those new dynamics, whether playing house, with dolls or action figures, team games, and so on. Whether structured or unstructured, kids are often learning a great deal with play, and most often it has very little to do with the "game" and more to do with interpersonal relations, their own inner dialog and feelings, and even physical movement and strengthening. Playing *is* learning.

Neuroscientists have discovered that play stimulates growth and development in the brain, and that it benefits the cerebral cortex (the part that governs higher cognitive function) even more than other parts of the brain. Play not only leads to higher IQ scores and cognitive abilities, it results in greater ability for linguistic learning and social development. It also encourages creativity and creative problem solving. Play in children also helps build impulse control and emotional regulation, leading to more social competency and empathy. Not to mention the physical fitness, agility, and dexterity often resulting from play.

That doesn't stop after childhood. Fun is still an alluring entree to deep learning.

Ask any teacher. Students learn better, more, and easier when they are having fun.

Good fantasies are fun because fun is so much more… well, *fun*. If you're not having a lot of fun in your fantasy, you're doing it wrong.

Now, as adults, our appreciation of fun is more nuanced, complex, and sometimes exotic. Bowling above

250, for instance, might not be all that interesting to a 5-year-old. Feeling genuine emotional as well as physical connection with an intimate partner might seem "from the outside" as only so stimulating (while "on the inside" there are fireworks). Speaking to a boardroom or audience well is a different kind of satisfying experience than child's play. But the depth and complexity and nuance don't change the fundamental dynamic that fun, enjoyment, pleasure, all aid in the learning process. Our brains are designed to learn from pleasure, as much as from pain.

So, the three qualities of good fantasies are:
1. Good fantasies are *specific*, rather than general.
2. Good fantasies lean heavily on *feelings*.
3. Good fantasies should be *fun*.

All you have to do in this second step of the process is follow your well-crafted suggestion with a fantasy of you achieving the goal or making the change that you desire. Really *enjoy* this.

Step Three – A Fantasy of Receiving the Benefits of Making the Change
The third step is similar to the second, in that it is a fantasy (so all the same advice about good fantasies applies), except that this second fantasy is one of you receiving the *benefits* of you having made the change or achieving the success. Whether that is closer connection with your spouse, the admiration of your friends (or competition), self-confidence, promotion at work, better grades, being respected by your boss… whatever. The benefits aren't just *one* thing, of course. The benefits can be as varied and numerous as the fantasies of success –

perhaps even more so, because for every success there are probably a number of benefits that result from it.

Again, really spend time tarrying with a few, specific, pleasurable benefits in each fantasy. Just as with the fantasy of success, you can have as many different fantasies of benefits as you like, as long as they are all centered around the goal you are wanting to reach, the change you are wanting to make. You don't have to cram in all the benefits of making the change into one fantasy – give yourself room to really bathe in each benefit.

Then, once the second fantasy has played itself through, simply return to your well-crafted suggestion, and begin again. It could be the same fantasy (or fantasies) over again, or a different one. As long as the fantasies are centered on the central change you want to make, you can have as many or as widely varied fantasies as you like.

This simple three-step practice deepens every time you cycle through, fantasy by fantasy, suggestion by suggestion, cycle by cycle. You'll likely find it easier after a few times doing it – humans do better with practice, generally, but creating an open and receptive state of mind is also a skill that can be developed and strengthened.

I recommend spending at least five minutes, three times a day, starting out. With practice, you may enjoy longer stretches of time, to spend longer in those satisfying fantasies. It is incredibly versatile, and can be used for a wide range of human experiences, goals, and changes. Once you've worked on an issue/goal/change for a while (a couple of weeks, at least), and you feel like you have reached that goal or made that change, then move to another goal or change you'd like to make. Imagine what you will look/feel/act like after a year of simply reprogramming yourself for the kind of lifestyle/attitude you want to have!

Trance formation is a skill that can be developed, and whose benefits extend into virtually every part of one's life. Freeing the Subconscious increases creativity and problem-solving. It boosts confidence and resilience – we can handle things easier because we are grounded and unshakably aware of our abundant personal resources. Trance training increases focus, making us more productive and efficient with our time, and our product more engaging and insightful. We are more motivated to do the things we need to do, to have the life we want to have, and chores seem less onerous because we can "trance into them" and *enjoy* that time. Also, the more we deal with our own issues, the more present we can be for other people in our lives: spouses, partners, kids, friends.... Trance formation is *transformative*.

The reality is that, as humans, we're going into hypnosis all the time, being influenced by whatever is around us or speaking to us at that moment. With intentional trance formation, we are not only deepening our openness to change or motivation, but also by selecting what influences us, we are deliberately shaping ourselves into the best version of ourselves. We don't have to react to the fear-mongering, the marketing/advertisement narrative of not being enough or not having enough. We are freed from the rush, the impatience, the hurry-up-catch-up rat race. Through transformative trance formation we gain perspective, understanding, and resolve. And that is golden.

I genuinely want that for you. And I'd love to hear what happens in your life as a result of it!

This is fundamentally different from simply "positive thinking" or "the law of attraction." We aren't naively glossing over difficulties or challenges. We aren't sending out waves to affect the material universe to manifest what we want out of thin air. (Though, it must be said, that *might* be happening in some way we aren't yet able to measure. I don't know. But it doesn't need to be the case for this technique to work.)

What we are doing is reprogramming the underlying patterns, scripts, expectations, reactions, assumptions, even our physical movements, that have in the past prevented us from being as successful as we have wanted to be. We are changing those subconscious/unconscious scripts into ones that *do* serve us in who we want to be! As we spoke about in the first two chapters, so much of our reactions and responses is based in unconscious programming that was created a long time ago, and might not be based in the best understanding of ourselves or the world. We don't often "look under the hood" to analyze the programming (its accuracy or usefulness) – we simply live our lives, reacting and responding because that's "the way things are."

One of the best insights to come out of Cognitive-Behavioral Therapy is a "transactional" understanding of stress. That is, stress is not simply an outside force affecting us. Stress is a transaction that takes place inside of us as we assess first the magnitude or quality of the "threat", and second as we assess our own ability to cope with that "threat" (our capacities, energy, knowledge, physical ability, emotional reserve, what have you). It is an interaction within ourselves that determines the level of "stress." That is why two people can have very similar experiences and have very different reactions to them. In the words of Shakespeare: "there is nothing either good or bad, but thinking makes it so." It is a philosophy that goes back at least as far as the Cynics in Classical Greece. And it is just as timely today: the recognition that experiences in our lives are *given* meaning, often unconsciously, and we respond to them *as if they were* that way.

The physics of bowling haven't changed. The dynamics in the meeting where you must give a presentation haven't changed. The actualities of child-birth haven't changed. But in all these cases, ideally, we can both reduce our perceived magnitude of the challenge, and increase our perceived abilities to cope with whatever challenge or change is before us. This isn't magic or pop-psychology. This isn't pollyannish or naive. This isn't wishful thinking. This is looking at how we are programmed – first by our environment and later by repeated experiences, then by our conscious and unconscious reflection on those experiences. Only now, we can take a direct role in what programming we adopt, what we allow to influence us. This technique merely takes advantage of some simple hacks that lie at the root of how we learn, how we affect that programming.

Of course, no simple at-home strategy should be seen as a replacement for professional help, if professional help is what is needed. If there is serious mental illness involved, then consultation with a licensed mental health provider is absolutely essential. If there are deep or enduring emotional or behavioral roadblocks (bad habits, thought patterns, etc.) that are "sub-clinical" (not at the level warranting a diagnosis), then help from a counselor, coach, or hypnotist might be helpful. For most of us, however, our problems are normal, everyday problems or challenges. In those cases, taking our programming into our own hands can be tremendously empowering, as insightful. That is where this technique comes in

One last suggestion. Before beginning this technique or practice, I recommend writing down at least seven measurable changes that accomplishing this goal will bring into your life. You know what you want to achieve (and if you don't, get clear on that first!). List out how your life will be different and better after having achieved that goal or having made that change. Make these benefits specific enough for you to know whether there has been progress made. Then, every week, revisit the list and notice any movement, any improvement.

This is important for two reasons. First, you want to be sure that you are making the change – and that is an awesome feeling you don't want to deny yourself. Sometimes we forget about our specific goals, or get fuzzy on the details, and it can be easy to miss the changes we've made because they seem so natural. Writing them down beforehand and revisiting them regularly will highlight the progress you are making.

Second, revisiting these benefits regularly will keep them in your mind (Conscious and Subconscious) and help integrate them into your awareness. You may see them throughout your day – in yourself or in others – and cultivate a deeper awareness of what you want to be or become. With this sort of work, as we work on one area of our lives, we often see our lives improve in other, unintended or surprising ways. It helps to be on the lookout for them

I have seen this practice work wonders – in the lives of my clients and in my own life. I use it myself! So I can unequivocally vouch for it. And soon, so will you.

Appendix

Is Hypnosis *Therapy*?

There are several words in our language and culture that play double-duty, that have an "official" (clinical, legal, proscribed) use or meaning, and also have currency in general, informal conversation. Sometimes the difference between the two isn't important, and sometimes it is very serious. Sometimes it is vitally important for the distinction to be made clear.

"Therapy" is one of these words that gets used a lot, in different contexts, to mean different things. There is an eccentric gift shop in Seattle called (literally) "Retail Therapy" but I'm almost certain no one goes in there expecting any formal therapeutic work to be done. At the same time, *therapy* is a legally protected term that only licensed practitioners (psychologists, counselors, psychiatrists, and so on) can use to describe their work. We all know that touch can be therapeutic, social interaction can be therapeutic, naps can be therapeutic, healthy diet and exercise can be therapeutic... but they aren't *therapy*. Oftentimes the difference is obvious (think of shopping at "Retail Therapy"). But with hypnosis, sometimes, the difference isn't as clear, and that lack of clarity can border on duplicity.

In Washington State, hypnosis for therapeutic ends is regulated by the state. If all I wanted to do was stage hypnosis – get people to sing like Elvis or bark like a dog for entertainment – then I wouldn't need to be registered. If, however, I intend to use hypnosis for the purpose of helping people achieve balance in their lives or effect the changes they want to make, essentially using it for therapeutic purposes, I must be registered and accountable to the state. In Washington State, I am registered legally as a "hypnotherapist" - the only state in the US that uses that language exclusively. But I most often describe myself simply as a "hypnotist" because I don't want to *imply* or give the *impression* of being something that I am not: specifically, a licensed mental health worker.

The word "therapy" generally means establishing or maintaining *balance* in one's life. And that's a great description of what most of us are trying to do in all sorts of ways. It is also a legal term that denotes a particular kind of professional relationship between a licensed provider and a patient, and includes a host of responsibilities and protections that aren't applicable in other relationships in our lives. That is why it is important for hypnotists of all stripes to be clear and up-front about our credentials and intentions. Part of that clarity is not taking advantage of the potential for misunderstanding of assumptions to give us more legal authority than we have.

So hypnosis, like many things, can be *therapeutic* – absolutely, especially if done with a skilled and ethical hypnotist in a professional setting. But unless hypnosis is done by a licensed provider in the context of therapy, it shouldn't be called *therapy* – and "hypnotherapy" has the dangerous potential (likelihood?) to be confusing or misleading in that regard. To be honest, I wouldn't expect most therapists who use hypnosis to call it "hypnotherapy" either, because it is only a tool used in the greater process of therapy. (No one uses "conversation-therapy" or "inviting-them-to-sit-down therapy.")

In recent years hypnotists and the psychological community have come to more-or-less an understanding reserving "hypnotherapy" for licensed providers only, even if (as in Washington State, for example) "hypnotherapy" is the legal category distinguishing it from hypnosis-for-entertainment. To maintain the not-for-entertainment distinction, some hypnotists have used the term "clinical hypnosis." But that hardly seems better to me.

I think the general public is savvy enough to distinguish the "hypnosis" I do in my office from the "hypnosis" you might find on the center stage of the state fair. I don't feel the need to emphasize my legal status as a "hypnotherapist" because it only invites confusion, especially given the ability for people in different states (and therefore under different laws or expectations) to find and contact me.

There are other words like this in everyday use, like "anxiety" and "depression." When clients describe themselves as having anxiety or depression, I'll almost always ask for clarification: is that a diagnosed disorder, or are you using that word to simply describe how you're feeling? The reality is that people use "anxiety" and "depression" all the time to refer to feelings or moods or behaviors that fall well below any diagnostic level. I use them myself in conversation with family and friends.

In a professional environment like hypnosis, however, we run into the same problem: am I implying the ability to diagnose a disorder by using terms that have potentially-diagnostic overtones? This is a delicate matter, indeed, because I don't want to discourage my clients from describing to me what they are feeling in their own words, and I don't want to give up the opportunity to speak to them in their own language, so to speak.

So there is a fine line that I actually find helpful to walk with my clients. Among licensed professionals (psychologists and counselors and the like), the terms "anxiety" and "depression" have very specific meaning. They use those words in the same way that massage therapists would identify specific muscles, or doctors specific regions of the brain. In conversation I might toss out the name of a muscle group or a term like "pre-frontal cortex", but it is probably clear that I'm not using them in the same way that a professional is. For those licensed mental health professionals, the words "anxiety" and "depression" fulfill certain diagnostic criteria and are followed by certain steps to take (or to avoid taking). When used by the general public, we simply don't mean this when using those words. We use them much more broadly, un-specifically, generally, sometimes as a catch-all buzz-word that could describe (or hide?) all kinds of feelings.

We often use anxiety to describe worry, fear, frustration, panic, a general sense of mistrust or suspicion, and a number of other emotional and even physical phenomena. Most of the time, when we talk about being "depressed" we mean something sub-clinical, like the blues, discouragement, being in a funk, fatigue, frustration, worry, and so on. These words, used in a general way, can point to a dizzying number of different feelings, emotions, and even "states." So those terms can just as often be distracting or distancing ourselves from talking about our feelings, as often as they are pointing us at what we are experiencing.

When working with clients, as much as possible, I like to dial in more specifically on *what* they are feeling. "When you say you feel anxious, what are you feeling? What does that feel like to you?" Or, even better: "If I were feeling what you are feeling when you're 'anxious,' what would I be experiencing?" If I were "depressed" in the same way you are, how would I know? With this kind of conversation we are able to dig deeper than the catch-all terms "anxiety" or "depression."

It isn't that those words aren't good words to use – however we describe our feelings is important and informative. But I find it helpful (and so do my clients!) to discern what precisely we're talking about. And since we don't typically use those terms in their specific, diagnostic sense, it is helpful to clarify what we are dealing with.

Can hypnosis help with depression or anxiety? Only if you're using those words in the common, sub-clinical vernacular. Diagnoses can only be given or "worked on" by a person licensed to give that diagnosis, or someone under their supervision. Most hypnotists are not licensed, and so are not legally (or ethically) able to address medical or psychological diagnoses. Hypnosis *can* help, however, with a lot of things. It is more helpful to think not in terms of "anxiety" or "depression", but rather in helping with mood, anger, frustration, sadness, worry, fear, and so on. Hypnosis, when done ethically and competently, is a professional service that is tremendously effective at helping normal, everyday people with normal, everyday problems.

So, is hypnosis *therapy*? In some general sense, yes, it is. But that language can be misleading, and making sure that it *isn't* misleading can require a few paragraphs to explain and make sure everyone is on the same page and understanding about the difference between licensure and sub-clinical helpful visualization and conversation. I find it easier to simply avoid the issue altogether by identifying what I do as hypnosis, leaving the therapy-question at the door. In the paperwork clients get (and are asked to read) it clarifies several times my legal and professional status, and distinguishes what I do (and what I will *not* do). That's usually more than enough.

I would have serious concerns about any hypnotist who leaned on using the term "hypnotherapy" (even in Washington State), or "clinical hypnosis," or used "depression" or "anxiety" (or any other "clinical" wording) to give an impression of licensure to an unsuspecting public.

Finding a good hypnotist is more than a matter of what *not* to list on a website, however. Since I imagine this book might be read across the United States, I would like to turn briefly to what to look *for* when looking for a hypnotist.

5 Things to Look for in a Hypnotist

It isn't uncommon, especially in these days of internet-personality, for people to claim fantastic things about themselves without any foundation or accountability. This is especially dangerous when those people are offering helping services – because unskilled or poorly done "help" can quickly turn to harm for their clients, and because it damages the reputation of everyone in the helping professions.

One of the biggest challenges to professional and *helping* hypnosis is that it is an unregulated industry. That is, there is no central authorizing or accrediting body whose singular responsibility it is to promote safe and effective practice, and monitor practitioner performance. While hypnosis is recognized as a legitimate and effective technique by the American Medical Association, the American Psychological Association, and the American Dental Association, there is no regulatory body that oversees its application and use generally.

Paradoxically, this is the way it should be. There shouldn't be a central authority for a phenomenon that every human being naturally possesses, and a technique that is present to some degree in virtually all communication. But, it does make for some awkward moments when talking about the formal practice of hypnotism.

That being said, I want to lay out some things for the lay person or potential client to look for when considering a hypnotist. My hope is to help people make informed decisions that will lead to safe, effective, reliable and healthy results for themselves and their loved ones when considering hypnosis as a helping modality.

1. Certification

Most hypnotists list among their credentials "Certified." As I mentioned above, there is no central certifying body regarding hypnosis. Any quick Google search will demonstrate this with startling vibrancy. There are literally dozens (perhaps hundreds) of ways to be "certified" as a hypnotist. Ranging from basic to rigorous, from legitimate to money-making "buy-a-diploma" scams, there is seemingly no end to options and grandiose claims by this organization or another.

In truth, in most states in the US, there is no legal requirement or credential at all for calling oneself a hypnotist. All one has to do is hang up their shingle and they are as "legitimate" as any other. (I know this because, not knowing any better, I inadvertently did this sort of thing after my first, elementary hypnosis certification. My first education in hypnosis didn't even acquaint me with the importance of rigorous standards in training and qualification!) One can call themselves "certified" or not, and it often doesn't make any sort of difference.

The question underlying certification is "*Who is doing the certifying?*" If you are investigating a hypnotist for services, and they claim a credential or other, ask who or what the credentialing body is.   Don't be impressed with names or titles of organizations – most of the impressive-sounding "bodies" are really just one person who created a "Board" to credential their own hypnosis curriculum or service.

If there is a single body that serves as a legitimate credentialing authority for non-clinical hypnosis (not associated with a licensed medical practice), it is the National Guild of Hypnotists. The National Guild is the oldest and largest professional hypnosis organization in the world, and is not run by, started by, or serving any *one* hypnosis school or individual. National Guild certification requires a minimum level of 100 contact hours of qualified instruction *and* annual continuing education. So if a hypnotist is certified by the Guild, you can expect a reliable level of proficiency, service, and professionalism.

Another body to look to is the Hypnotherapists Union (OPEIU Guild 104, AFL-CIO), which also requires 100 hours of qualified training to be a member, but I don't find many hypnotists or hypnotherapists referencing their union membership. There are also other, smaller, more local hypnosis/hypnotherapy unions in geographic areas with a particular concentration of hypnotists, with their own rules and requirements for membership, but these are not the national union I am referring to here.

Now, there may be other credentialing bodies out there that just as nobly serve practitioners and clients as the National Guild, but I don't know about them. If your potential hypnotist claims certification from anyone other than the National Guild of Hypnotists, it is cause for further investigation. They could be totally legit... you just need to dig a little deeper.

In that case, ask for their particular qualifications and experience. What school/program did they attend? What kind of training was it – in-person or online, live or recorded? Did they have supervised clinical hours/practice?

Another element here is "certification" versus "re-certification." One-time certifications should raise red-flags – not that they aren't legitimate (college degrees are, after all, examples of one-time certifications), but just that they might be diploma-mill products. (My first two hypnosis certifications were, in fact, one-time non-renewables. They were good for what they were, but I wouldn't want to be hypnotized by someone relying on them.) The National Guild of Hypnotists (among others) requires annual re-certification, which ensures ethical and professional excellence. Make sure your hypnotist is currently Guild certified, or current with whatever credentialing body they reference. One simple way to do this is to contact the National Guild itself, asking for qualified/certified/credentialed hypnotists in your area.

One more consideration is "Board Certification." There are organizations who call themselves the Board of this or that, and then bestow "Board Certification" on their members. Genuine Board Certification (as you will find in the NGH) is an advanced level of certification, above and beyond "Certification." Board certification, for it to mean anything, must include what is expected with that title: so many years of experience, demonstrated ethical and professional excellence, a rigorous exam to objectively measure knowledge, significant published work on hypnosis, continued education and a contribution to the further development of the profession as a whole, and importantly a paneled interview of representatives of the governing Board. Board certification in the NGH is impressive and important precisely because it requires so much more than basic certification. If someone describes their credentials as "Board Certified," it is worth asking what that means (and by whom). The answer should be informative, either way.

Certification by the National Guild of Hypnotists is a good benchmark for basic qualifications. There are many different schools (of hypnosis training, of hypnosis thought) that offer training that leads to NGH certification. (As I said, the NGH isn't owned by one person or school.) If someone *isn't* certified by the Guild, they still may be a good hypnotist, simply more questions need to be asked. If someone *is* NGH certified, then you can begin to explore the other training, experience and expertise they bring to their practice.

2. Techniques

Hypnosis is as diverse as there are hypnotists, and there are innumerable different "techniques" or methods or tools or procedures that one can use in the practice of hypnosis. Some require more training than others. Some are more effective than others in different situations.

What you want in a hypnotist is more than just "Direct Suggestion" and "Guided Imagery." Those techniques are good so far as they go... but they only scratch the surface of what hypnosis is capable of. Moreover, their effects tend to be short-lived, because the root cause of the problem has not been addressed.

I would highly recommend looking for a hypnotist or hypnotherapist who practices insight-based therapies – techniques and procedures that seek genuine insight, and go after root cause. Minimally, I would recommend a hypnotist proficient in Age Regression and Progression, Parts Therapy and Chair Therapy. You don't need to know what those are - you just need to know if your hypnotist takes an insight-based approach. A note of caution: the National Guild of Hypnotists requires additional, advanced training for hypnotists practicing in any of three areas - working with children, pain management, or age regression. If someone is certified by the Guild, and they are practicing age regression, they should have had qualified, advanced training. If someone isn't certified by the Guild, then specific questions about training for the techniques they use is wise.

Guided imagery, analogy, metaphor and direct suggestion are good for short-term/temporary effects, because they are good at "softening" the "hardened" mind

– but they don't fundamentally change the underlying problem. More radical and far-reaching techniques (for examples, age regression or "parts work") go to the root association of the problem behavior/belief and change it with the insight and understanding of the whole/adult/best person.

The point is that many hypnotists rely on very light-level therapeutic techniques – which are fine when used in concert with more powerful and transformative techniques, but alone do not provide the level of change and lasting effect hypnosis is capable of.

3. Advanced Training

We all want a hypnotist at the top of their game. This requires not only the best education starting off, but continual professional advancement and continuing education. (I mentioned earlier that membership in the Guild is predicated on a minimum level of annual continuing education. This is another reason why Guild membership is the Gold Standard for certification.)

There is an abundance of very good advanced training and education available to qualified hypnotists. The National Guild, for instance, goes to great effort to encourage and promote excellent continuing education. This is training *in addition to* the basic training required for membership in the Guild. I mentioned above the option of Board certification in the NGH, which is worth looking for when weighing options (but whose absence doesn't mean anything bad about the hypnotist – Board certification is difficult and time-consuming, or they may just not choose to announce it for their own reasons).

Among the most advanced and (in my opinion) best training is 5-PATH® certification. 5-PATH® stands for "Five Phase Advanced Transformational Hypnosis," and it systematizes the most effective tools for hypnosis for greatest efficacy. I have had this training, so I can personally vouch for the quality of the training. I highly recommend seeking out a hypnotist with 5-PATH® certification.

Another advanced training I can personally recommend is that required to become a teacher of 7th Path Self-Hypnosis. 7th Path Self-Hypnosis is unique in that it is the only self-hypnosis program that actively seeks out and neutralizes negative or erroneous programming in our subconscious. Instead of just offering affirmations that paper over the underlying issues, 7th Path works to rid ourselves of the root causes of our problem behaviors or beliefs, while at the same time helping us re-program our Subconscious for the kind of life we want to live. Becoming a 7th Path Self-Hypnosis teacher isn't difficult, but it does add depth and endurance to any hypnosis process. If you can find a hypnotist trained in both 5-PATH® and 7th Path Self-Hypnosis, I would be very surprised if you found your time with them anything less than profoundly transformative.

The point here is that there is additional training beyond basic certification (by the Guild or anyone else). But what you want to make sure of is that this training is *in addition to* qualified basic education – not in lieu of it.

4. "Systematic" versus "Client-Centered"

Unsurprisingly, there is a spectrum of approaches to hypnosis. "Systematic" denotes that the hypnotist has a particular system, process or pattern that she leans on in her practice. These usually are fairly general, outlining a process whose specific content is provided by the client and their issue.

"Client-Centered" points to a philosophy that the client steers the work in the direction they choose. This isn't absolute, of course, because the best "client-centered" hypnotists have a wealth of experience, knowledge and tools to draw on, to offer the client, and to guide with. But in contrast with the systematic practitioners, client-centered hypnotherapists don't have a pre-planned process, route or procedure for a client before meeting with them.

Both types of hypnosis are valid and good, with their advantages and disadvantages. In reality, of course, no hypnotist is at either extreme. Even the most dedicated systematic hypnotist leaves room for client response and engagement. Even the most client-centered hypnotist has some idea of what might best serve a client with a given problem – that expertise is exactly why people seek out qualified hypnotists. The preference really comes down to the personality (and perhaps training) of the individual hypnotist and their individual client.

For instance, I lean towards a systematic approach, since I like being confident about the journey the client will go on, the benchmarks I know I have to meet before proceeding to the next step, and the consistency of the tools and techniques I employ. The actual content of every session will vary widely from any other, based on the client's contribution and the "step in the process" we find ourselves. That having been said, every client is an individual, and I find that responding to those variables a healthy challenge and a delight. I have a roadmap I like to use, but sometimes our journey takes us elsewhere.

The point is that different hypnotists do hypnosis differently. When exploring hypnotists in your area, it might be good to have a conversation with them not just about *techniques* but about their *philosophy* about hypnosis, and how you as the client fit into it. In any case, you should be convinced that they have your best interests at heart, are able to respond to your individuality, and have the experience and expertise to give you the product you seek: a healthier, happier you.

5. **Rapport**

It may seem intuitive, but it is important enough to emphasize here: you should jive well with your hypnotist. You should implicitly trust her – her manner of speaking, her training and methodology, her intentions and goals. You should enjoy the sound of her voice (she'll probably speak slightly differently during formal hypnosis, but you'll probably like it even more then). You should feel good around her. You should be confident that she is professional, in the very best sense of the word.

Hypnosis is all about *trust*, and if you have any misgivings or doubts or heebie-jeebies about her, then consider looking for a different hypnotist. There is no shame in having consultations or conversations with several hypnotists to find the right one for you. You shouldn't feel any pressure to sign up or commit right then. (If you want to commit right then, they should be prepared to act on your enthusiasm!)

Rapport isn't just desirable for good hypnosis – it is absolutely essential. If you are distracted by concerns or mistrust, you're not going to be able to fully engage in the process. There will be a part of you always holding back. Hypnosis works best when you're all in. (You always maintain control of yourself, and will reject any suggestions inconsistent with your values, morals or intentions.) Having a good relationship with your hypnotist is important. If you get any feeling like that might be an issue, don't ignore it. Trust your instincts!

I really believe in hypnosis – I've seen amazing transformations in my office and in my own life. Every day I am in awe of the human mind and its power. I hope that if you are interested in exploring hypnosis to help you, that these five guideposts will help you find the perfect hypnotist for you. You are worth it.

About the Author

Christian Skoorsmith is an award-winning hypnotist, author, teacher, and sought-after speaker to national and international audiences on hypnosis. He is a Board Certified Hypnotist in full-time private practice, and a Certified Hypnosis Instructor with the National Guild of Hypnotists (NGH). He is a regular contributor to *The Journal of Hypnotism* (NGH) and *The 5-PATH® Journal* (International Association of Hypnosis Professionals), as well as frequent speaker in the US, Europe and Australia. In addition to serving on the Advisory Board of the IAHP, Christian is also adjunct faculty at the NGH international education conference. He currently lives with his partner and children in Seattle, Washington. He is the highest-rated hypnotist in Seattle, and was named among the "Top 3" Hypnotists in Seattle in 2019, 2020, 2021, and 2022. The IAHP awarded him the Self-Hypnosis instruction excellence award in 2021, and recognized his contribution to evidence-based hypnosis with the Science award that same year. In 2022, the NGH recognized his work on applications for Tinnitus with the Hypnotism Research Award. Christian spends as much time as he can carving an off-grid homestead out of the Pacific Northwest rainforest, raising three children with his wife, and is also a professional whisky nose, a fan of Robert Burns poetry, and an ok bagpiper.

You can find more about Christian on his website at www.WholeHealth.today, or follow him on Facebook at www.facebook.com/christian.skoorsmith.35 and www.facebook.com/WholeHealthHypnosis.